© by Johan Labuschagne except for the part by Andrew Murray on Humility. All rights reserved and no copying in any form is allowed without the permission by the author.
All scriptures used are from the King James Version or the New King James Version of the bible as found on e-Sword ® 10.0.07, Copyright © 2000 -2012, Rick Meyers

First Edition

ISBN 979-0-620-71850-9

Table of contents

- My story and journey with Pride

- The origin of Pride
    - Satan and his fall
    - Satan in disguise
    - Leviathan
- The Symptoms / Manifestations of Pride
    - Achievements of self and others
    - Adopting another persona / image
    - Adultery
    - Always late
    - Anger
    - Being Argumentative
    - Arrogance
    - Atheism
    - Center of attention
    - Claiming God's and other people's credit
    - Comparisons and competition
    - Unable to give compliments
    - Control, manipulation and power
    - Critical spirit
    - The desire for power and riches
    - Disloyalty
    - Division / Denominations / Divorce
    - Envy / Jealousy and Strife
    - Fear and worry
    - Gossip
    - Humour and Sarcasm

- Idolatry
- Impatience and irritability
- Judgement
- Lack of a submissive attitude
- Lying
- More invested in being heard, than in hearing
- My way
- Babbling
- People pleasing
- Perfectionism
- Racism
- Rebellion
- Revenge
- Self-centeredness, Self-obsession and Self-pity
- Shyness
- Stealing
- Stinginess vs Giving
- Stubbornness
- Unforgiveness and bitterness
- Ungratefulness
- Unteachable spirit
- The Slumbering spirit
-

* Humility by Andrew Murray
  - Chapter 1. The Glory of the Creature
  - Chapter 2. The Secret of Redemption
  - Chapter 3. Humility in the life of Jesus

- Chapter 4. Humility in the Teaching of Jesus
- Chapter 5. Humility in the Disciples of Jesus
- Chapter 6. Humility in Daily life
- Chapter 7. Humility and Holiness
- Chapter 8. Humility and Sin
- Chapter 9. Humility and Faith
- Chapter 10. Humility and the death to Self
- Chapter 11. Humility and Happiness
- Chapter 12. Humility and Exaltation

Pride

My story and journey with Pride

I grew up in a 'Christian' home. We were in a Reformed Protestant church, although attending church very seldom. When I attended high school, I went through the church catechism. Nowhere was it mentioned, that to be brought up in a 'Christian' home was not a free pass to heaven and an intimate relationship with God. Nowhere was it said that you have to be converted and then be baptized. The fact that you were born in a Christian home and baptized as a baby, not even aware what was going on, was good enough and a sure road to the Promised Land.

It was only later when I went to university that I was confronted with different views about my faith that I started thinking more seriously about these matters.

I read some books by Watchmen Nee and began to understand there was more to the Holy Scriptures than what you superficially read when you casually glance at the script. I remember I was bit angry / jealous / envious. How can a Chinese, not growing up in a 'Christian country' know so much, not even growing up in a 'Christian environment? How can 'we' growing up in a 'Christian' environment and even attending 'Christian schools' be so ignorant and missed so much?

I began to understand that there was more to the blood of Christ and baptism than simply dying on the cross and the quick sprinkling of water. During that time, I was searching, attending various churches but could not find what satisfied my spiritual needs.

I eventually got married to a woman with the same spiritual background as me, and so we happily followed the same path that we were brought up in. We had a one child (a boy) which we also had baptized as a baby, and so the iniquities of the fathers were passed on down the line. Never explaining the importance of a personal decision to follow Christ. Basking in the fantasy that I was baptized as a baby and grew up in a 'Christian' home, going on from one generation to the next and Hallelujah we will pass through the pearly gates. Acts 2:38 clearly states: 'Repent and be baptized'.

I was really converted in 2006. It was during a time in my life where I was honestly trying to go deeper in my spiritual walk. I was attending church more regularly but always felt there was something more than just sitting in a pew on a Sunday, and the rest of the week would go on as if there was no God. I earnestly started to pray that God would take away this ceiling I felt I was praying against. One day at church I saw a poster against a noticeboard that advertised a course over a period of 10 weeks, once a week, that one could attend, and it would be about the Holy Spirit, and it was free. At that time, I was able to attend this course which was in the morning during weekdays. The teacher was a former minister in the denomination I was in then, but by that time he had his own ministry detached from any denomination for about 12 years. During that 10-week course he started to explain the workings of the Holy Spirit and showed how it operated from early in the Old Testament already, right through the New

Testament up to the present day. When the course was over the minister asked if there were people who want to commit their lives to the Lord and be baptized. They can make a date and come to his house which had a swimming pool. About have of the attendees did that, although I think all were from the denomination I was in then, who mainly baptized babies by sprinkling water on them rather than adults who made an informed decision, and then being submersed in water. So we were all baptized a second time. First as babies in our denomination, and then after our 'conversion' and personal choice. This was a clear turning point in our lives.

I have always been aware that it was difficult for me to apologize or ask for forgiveness. I've always had the urge, when I knew I offended someone or did them wrong, to go and look them in the face and apologize. I never understood why. Why was it easy for some people to open and honestly ask for forgiveness, but not for me? I would sometimes go to people with the explicit purpose to do that, but when I face them, it was like someone was choking me and words would not come out.

My family has a very strong 'pride tradition'. Never in my childhood-home have I ever heard someone admitting they made a mistake and apologizing nor asking forgiveness for it. That example was the one I followed.

After my conversion, two bible verses kept haunting me: 1Peter 5:5 'Likewise, ye younger, submit yourselves unto the elder. Yea, all of you be subject one to another, and be clothed with humility: for God resisteth the proud, and giveth grace to the humble.'

Deep inside of me I knew the root was pride, but I had no clue how to deal with it.
The other scripture that was gnawing me was: Mat 6:14-15. 'For if ye forgive men their trespasses, your heavenly Father will also forgive you: 15 But if ye forgive not men their trespasses, neither will your Father forgive your trespasses.'

I realized that if the most powerful force in the universe was resisting me because of my pride, what chance did I have to a personal and intimate relationship with Him. I also found it hard to forgive people who wronged me, so here I had another thorn in the flesh. Because I can't forgive, God can't forgive me. I had double trouble.

Not long after my conversion a friend introduced me to a Holy Spirit ministry. It was not a church or denomination. One had to pay to do the course, and it was held at various places across the country. The teachings were in the form of DVD's and on various topics like: marriage, and yes, forgiveness and pride inter alia. Here I got confronted with the realities of this evil and slowly with the help of the Holy Spirit and prayer, I came to a deeper understanding of these evils and started to deal with it. Let me state it clearly, I don't think we ever 'arrive' and conquer it completely. I certainly haven't arrived yet, and can imagine that it will be a live-long struggle without totally eradicating this evil. What has happened is that I became aware of the subtlety and the various heads of this snake called pride, and can at least distinguish between its various disguised forms and repent about it and move on. It has certainly brought me to the point where I can honestly look someone in the face and apologize and ask forgiveness, than it was before.

My journey on this path started after my divorce. After coming to a better understanding of pride, I could go back to my wife and son and apologize and ask forgiveness for my part in the hurt caused by the divorce. The reason for the divorce did certainly not only come from my side and was not due to drinking with friends late at night, beating or fighting with my wife. I could have easily reasoned that we both had equal part in this divorce, so that equaled things out and we were square. But having gained a deeper understanding of pride and healing, I knew if I didn't ask for forgiveness the spiritual wounds would not be healed, even though the other parties might not have understood the reason why I did it, I believe it also brought healing and closure to them.

Walking around with pride and unforgiveness in our hearts can make us physically and emotionally sick. It is a known fact in the medical field that many physical illnesses are the results of emotional and spiritual unbalance. In other words the medical field deals a lot with, and tries to cure the manifestations and symptoms of our inner turmoil and wrestling, that manifests physically in our bodies.

The origin of Pride

Satan and his fall

We read about Satan's cunning ways in the oldest book in the Bible: Job 1:8 'And Jehovah said to Satan, Have you set your heart against My servant Job, because there is none like him in the earth, a perfect and upright man, one who fears God and turns away from evil?'

We also read in the first book in the bible (Genesis) how Eve was tempted by Satan and misled Adam and Eve after God told them NOT to eat from the tree of knowledge of good and evil: Gen 2:9 'And out of the ground Jehovah God caused to grow every tree that is pleasant to the sight, and good for food. The tree of life also was in the middle of the garden, and the tree of knowledge of good and evil.'

Gen 2:17 'but you shall not eat of the tree of knowledge of good and evil. For in the day that you eat of it you shall surely die.'

We know that Eve was misled by Satan, and in Adam's presence, ate of the forbidden fruit. Gen 3:17 'And to Adam He said, Because you have listened to the voice of your wife and have eaten of the tree, of which I commanded you, saying, You shall not eat of it! The ground is cursed for your sake. In pain shall you eat of it all the days of your life.'

We read in Isaiah 14 how Satan, a created being and an angel lifted himself up against God because he became full of pride. Someone once said the problem with *sin*, is the I in the middle of the word sIn. It's all about ME, the I. I want this, I deserve that. Why can he/she have it, and I must go without? Take note of the five I's in Satan's reasoning in Isaiah.

Isa 14:11 'Your pride is brought down to the grave, and the noise of your harps. The maggot is spread under you, and the worms cover you. :12 How you are fallen from the heavens, O shining star, son of the morning! How you are cut down to the ground, you who weakened the nations! :13 For you have said in your heart, I will go up to the heavens, I will exalt my throne above the stars of God; I will also sit on the mount of the congregation, in the sides of the north. :14 I will go up above the heights of the clouds; I will be like the Most High.' Satan wanted to be like the Most High.

It appears that there were other angels that sided with the Devil and that about a third of them were cast out of heaven into the earth with Satan. Rev 12:3 'And another sign was seen in the heavens. And behold a great red dragon, having seven heads and ten horns and seven crowns on his heads! :4 And his tail drew the third part of the stars of heaven, and cast them onto the earth. And the dragon stood before the woman being about to bear, so that when she bears, he might devour her child.'

Satan's fellow angels are also called minions and are highly organized, and specialize in various areas of sin and temptation. Paul talks about powers, principalities and rulers of darkness. Eph 6:12 'For we wrestle not against flesh and blood, but against principalities, against powers, against the rulers of the darkness of this world, against spiritual wickedness in high places.' Some

translations use the word 'governments' in this verse. To have principalities and rulers, you have to have a structure, and organization to implement and carry out your plans. Jesus himself talked about Satan's kingdom which implies a system. Mat 12:26 'And if Satan cast out Satan, he is divided against himself; how shall then his kingdom stand?'
Kingdoms, like God's kingdom is organized. In Satan's kingdom there certainly is structure, organization and rulers of principalities (areas and cities) with responsibilities and tasks. I believe this system is run on fear and punishment. Every subject must perform or be punished. A performance-based system.

Paul also calls Satan 'the god of this world' and the one who blinds people from the gospel of Christ. 2Co 4:4 'in whom the god of this world has blinded the minds of the unbelieving ones, so that the light of the glorious gospel of Christ (who is the image of God) should not dawn on them.'

Satan in disguise

We see that in the garden of Eden Satan sowed doubt and changed his appearance. He came as a serpent, one of the many of his clever tactics he practices to this day. Gen 3:1 'Now the serpent was more cunning than any beast of the field which Jehovah God had made. And he said to the woman, Is it so that God has said, You shall not eat of every tree of the garden? :2 And the woman said to the serpent, We may eat of the fruit of the trees of the garden. :3 But of the fruit of the tree which is in the middle of the garden, God has said, You shall not eat of it, neither shall you touch it, lest you die. :5 for God knows that in the day you eat of it, then your eyes shall be opened, and you shall be as God, knowing good and evil.'

It also is clear that Satan is an active being and always looking for work. This we see in Job 1:6 'Now there was a day when the sons of God came to present themselves before the LORD, and Satan came also among them. :7 And the LORD said unto Satan, Whence comest thou? Then Satan answered the LORD, and said, From going to and fro in the earth, and from walking up and down in it.'

He appears restless and has no peace.

Satan will always come in disguise. If Satan came walking towards you looking like an illustration in the Children's bible (with horns on his head and a fork in his hand) you would certainly laugh and tell him to go play somewhere else. He is more cunning and shrewd than that. The end-result of what he offers you will always appear to be to your benefit. In the short term at least.

Leviathan

In Job 41 we read about the nature and characteristics of Satan / Lucifer / the Devil. Here he is described as an animal called 'Leviathan'. The Strong dictionary defines it as follows:
H3867; 'a wreathed animal, that is, a serpent (especially the crocodile or some other large sea monster); figuratively the constellation of the

dragon; also, as a symbol of Babylon: - leviathan, mourning.'

I think it is important to look at the whole chapter about this monster:

Job 41:1 'Can you draw out the leviathan with a hook, or hold down his tongue with a cord? :2 Can you put a reed rope into his nose, or pierce his jaw with a thorn? :3 Will he multiply pleas for help to you? Will he speak soft words to you? :4 Will he make a covenant with you? Will you take him for a servant for ever? :5 Will you play with him as with a bird? Or will you bind him for your maidens? :6 Shall your companions bargain over him? Shall they divide him among the merchants? :7 Can you fill his skin with barbed irons, or his head with fishing spears? :8 Lay your hand on him, think of the battle; you will never do it again. :9 Behold, his hope has been made false; will not one be cast down at the sight of him? :10 None is so fierce as to dare to stir him up; who then is able to stand before Me? :11 Who has gone before Me that I should repay? All that is the heavens is Mine. :12 I will not keep silent concerning his limbs, or his mighty strength, or the grace of his frame. :13 Who can take off the surface of his skin; who can come to him with his double bridle? :14 Who can open the doors to his face? Terror is round about his teeth. :15 The rows of shields are his pride, shut up with a close seal; :16 one is so near to another that no air can come between them; :17 they are joined one to another, they clasp each other so that they can not be separated. :18 His sneezings flash forth light, and his eyes are like the eyelids of the dawn. :19 Out of his mouth go burning torches, sparks of fire leap out. :20 Out of his nostrils goes smoke, as out of a boiling pot fired by reeds. :21 His breath kindles coals, and a flame goes out of his mouth. :22 In his neck remains strength, and terror dances before him. :23 The folds of his flesh are joined together, cast firm on him; he cannot be moved.

:24 His heart is cast hard as a stone, even cast hard as a piece of a riding millstone :25 The mighty are afraid from his rising; they are beside themselves from the crashing. :26 The sword overtakes him, but will not hold firm. The spear, the dart, and the javelin also. :27 He counts iron as straw, bronze as rotten wood. :28 An arrow cannot make him flee; slingstones are turned by him into stubble. :29 Darts are counted as straw; he laughs at the shaking of a javelin. :30 Points of potsherds are under him; he spreads sharp pointed marks on the mire. :31 He makes the deep boil like a pot; he makes the sea like a pot of ointment. :32 He makes a path to shine after him; one would think the deep to be gray-headed. :33 On earth there is nothing like him, one made without fear. :34 He beholds all high things; **he is a king over all the sons of pride.**'

The Symptoms / Manifestations of Pride

As said before, the deceiver (Satan) works in ways which are not easily recognized.
It is like most diseases / illnesses. You might have a headache, and taking pills for it only helps for a while, then one has to take another pill, until the root (cause) of the problem has been addressed, and then healing comes. And so a spiritual 'symptom' might appear in someone and we desperately want to fix it, but the problem persists maybe for the rest of someone's live, or until they,

or someone identifies the root problem and delivers the person of that spirit. Because Satan is a spiritual being, he enters us on a spiritual level.

There is a general believe amongst Christians that all sins have its root in Pride. This was the original sin out if which all others sin flow. Someone said that Pride is like bad breath. Everyone is aware of it, except the one with the 'smelly voice'.

Something that is so easy spotted in others, and yet so difficult to see in ourselves. Most people think pride is restricted to a 'haughty' look, or people who clearly act and talk down to, and about other people. That is exactly what Satan wants us to believe leaving a wide range of opportunities to continue his dirty work.

A quick search on e-sword (KJV) on: *the spirit of…* renders the following result.

Num 5:14 'And the *spirit of jealousy* come upon him, and he be jealous of his wife, and she be defiled: or if the spirit of jealousy come upon him, and he be jealous of his wife, and she be not defiled:'

Deu 34:9 'And Joshua the son of Nun was full of the *spirit of wisdom*; for Moses had laid his hands upon him: and the children of Israel hearkened unto him, and did as the LORD commanded Moses.'

Here is a sign of the transference of a spirit from Moses to Joshua.

1Sa 1:15 'And Hannah answered and said, No, my lord, I am a woman of *a sorrowful spirit*: I have drunk neither wine nor strong drink, but have poured out my soul before the LORD.'

Sa 28:7 'Then said Saul unto his servants, Seek me a woman that hath *a familiar spirit,* that I may go to her, and enquire of her. And his servants said to him, Behold, there is a woman that hath a familiar spirit at Endor.'

1Ki 22:23 'Now therefore, behold, the LORD hath put *a lying spirit* in the mouth of all these thy prophets, and the LORD hath spoken evil concerning thee.'

Pro 11:13 'A talebearer revealeth secrets: but he that is of *a faithful spirit* concealeth the matter.'

Pro 16:19 'Better it is to be of an *humble spirit* with the lowly, than to divide the spoil with the proud.'

Pro 17:27 'He that hath knowledge spareth his words: and a man of understanding is of *an excellent spirit.*'

Pro 18:14 'The spirit of a man will sustain his infirmity; but *a wounded spirit* who can bear?'

Ecc 7:8 'Better is the end of a thing than the beginning thereof: *and* the patient in spirit *is* better than *the proud in spirit.*'

Ecc 7:9 'Be not hasty in *thy spirit to be angry*: for anger resteth in the bosom of fools.'

Isa 4:4 'When the Lord shall have washed away the filth of the daughters of Zion, and shall have purged the blood of Jerusalem from the midst thereof by *the spirit of judgment*, and by the *spirit of burning*.'

Isa 11:2 'And the spirit of the LORD shall rest upon him*, the spirit of wisdom and understanding, the spirit of counsel and might, the spirit of knowledge and of the fear of the LORD.*'

Wow! Aren't these the spirits we must ask the Lord to activate in us every day?

Isa 19:3 'And *the spirit of Egypt* shall fail in the midst thereof; and I will destroy the counsel thereof: and they shall seek to the idols, and to the charmers, and to them that have *familiar spirits*, and to the wizard.'

Isa 29:10 'For the LORD hath poured out upon you *the spirit of deep sleep*, and hath closed your eyes: the prophets and your rulers, the seers hath he covered.'

Isa 61:3 'To appoint unto them that mourn in Zion, to give unto them beauty for ashes, the oil of joy for mourning, the garment of praise for *the spirit of heaviness*; that they might be called trees of righteousness, the planting of the LORD, that he might be glorified.'

Isa 66:2 'For all those things hath mine hand made, and all those things have been, saith the LORD: but to this man will I look, even to him that is poor and of *a contrite spirit*, and trembleth at my word.'

Hos 4:12 'My people ask counsel at their stocks, and their staff declareth unto them: for *the spirit of whoredoms* hath caused them to err, and they have gone a whoring from under their God.'

Zec 12:10 'And I will pour upon the house of David, and upon the inhabitants of Jerusalem, *the spirit of grace and of supplications*: and they shall look upon me whom they have pierced, and they shall mourn for him, as one mourneth for his only son, and shall be in bitterness for him, as one that is in bitterness for his firstborn.'

Mar 5:2 'And when he was come out of the ship, immediately there met him out of the tombs a man with *an unclean spirit*,'

Mar 9:25 'When Jesus saw that the people came running together, he rebuked the *foul spirit*, saying unto him, Thou *dumb and deaf spirit*, I charge thee, come out of him, and enter no more into him.'

Luk 4:33 'And in the synagogue there was a man, which had *a spirit of an unclean devil*, and cried out with a loud voice.'

Luk 13:11 'And, behold, there was a woman which had *a spirit of infirmity* eighteen years, and was bowed together, and could in no wise lift up herself.'

Joh 14:17 'Even *the Spirit of truth*; whom the world cannot receive, because it seeth him not, neither knoweth him: but ye know him; for he dwelleth with you, and shall be in you.'

Act 16:16 'And it came to pass, as we went to prayer, a certain damsel possessed with *a spirit of divination* met us, which brought her masters much gain by soothsaying:'

Rom 1:4 'And declared *to be* the Son of God with power, according to *the spirit of holiness*, by the resurrection from the dead:'

Rom 8:15 'For ye have not received *the spirit of bondage* again to fear; but ye have received the *Spirit of adoption*, whereby we cry, Abba, Father.'

Rom 11:8 '(According as it is written, God hath given them *the spirit of slumber*, eyes that they should not see, and ears that they should not hear;) unto this day.'

1Co 2:12 'Now we have received, not the _spirit of the world_, but _the spirit which is of God_; that we might know the things that are freely given to us of God.'

1Co 4:21 'What will ye? shall I come unto you with a rod, or in love, and in the _spirit of meekness?_'

2Co 4:13 'We having the same _spirit of faith_, according as it is written, I believed, and therefore have I spoken; we also believe, and therefore speak.'

Eph 1:17 'That the God of our Lord Jesus Christ, the Father of glory, may give unto you _the spirit of wisdom and revelation_ in the knowledge of him:'

Eph 2:2 'Wherein in time past ye walked according to the course of this world, according to the prince of the power of the air_, the spirit that now worketh in the children of disobedience:_'

2Ti 1:7 'For God hath not given us _the spirit of fear_, but _of power_, and _of love_, and _of a sound mind._'

1Pe 3:4 'But let it be the hidden man of the heart, in that which is not corruptible, even the ornament of _a meek and quiet spirit_, which is in the sight of God of great price.'

1Pe 4:14 'If ye be reproached for the name of Christ, happy are ye; _for the spirit of glory_ and of God resteth upon you: on their part he is evil spoken of, but on your part he is glorified.'

1Jn 4:3 'And every spirit that confesseth not that Jesus Christ is come in the flesh is not of God: and this is _that spirit of antichrist_, whereof ye have heard that it should come; and even now already is it in the world.'

1Jn 4:6 'We are of God: he that knoweth God heareth us; he that is not of God heareth not us. Hereby know we _the spirit of truth_, and _the spirit of error_.'

Rev 19:10 'And I fell at his feet to worship him. And he said unto me, See thou do it not: I am thy fellow servant, and of thy brethren that have the testimony of Jesus: worship God: for the testimony of Jesus is _the spirit of prophecy_.'

The Strong definition of spirit is:
G4151

πνεῦμα

pneuma

pnyoo'-mah

From G4154; a _current_ of air, that is, _breath_ (_blast_) or a _breeze_; by analogy or figuratively a _spirit_, that is, (human) the rational _soul_, (by implication) _vital principle_, mental _disposition_, etc., or (superhuman) an _angel_, _daemon_, or (divine) God, Christ's _spirit_, the Holy _spirit_: - ghost, life, spirit (-ual, -ually), mind

The English word 'pneumatic' comes from the root Greek word 'pneuma'. Pneumatic is air power. Some power tools work on air pressure / power, like drills, jackhammers etc.

It is like breath, wind or air. Something that can't be seen with the naked eye, but has definite power.

Unfortunately, few preachers point this out to their flock and a _spirit of slumber_ come over them and they never achieve true victory in their spiritual walk with God. We open ourselves for these spirits (evil or good) to enter us, but we can with the authority we have in Jesus's blood, and His victory on the cross, cast out the evil spirits in Jesus Name. So that we can be free and live as overcomers and not been knee- strapped by these spirits.

We have authority over these spirits according to Jesus: Luk 10:20 'Yet do not rejoice in this, that the evil spirits are subject to you, rather rejoice because your names are written in Heaven.'

The apostle Paul encountered a woman with an unclean spirit and he identified the spirit and cast it out. Act 16:16 'And it came to pass, as we went to prayer, a certain damsel possessed with a spirit of divination met us, which brought her masters much gain by soothsaying: :17 The same followed Paul and us, and cried, saying, These men are the servants of the most high God, which shew unto us the way of salvation. :18 And this did she many days. But Paul, being grieved, turned and said to the spirit, I command thee in the name of Jesus Christ to come out of her. And he came out the same hour.'

Following are some of the ways Pride manifests itself in our lives. This is by no means a final and comprehensive list of these manifestations but can be used in bible study groups, church cell groups or house churches where members can discuss and reveal these phenomena. More than often people would start adding or expanding on these matters and even confess that they are been plagued by such spirits, then other members could

minister to them if they agree to it. Prayer with the laying on of hands is always wonderful way of ministering to such people. The spirit is commanded to go in the name of Jesus (Yeshua) to dry places where Jesus / Yeshua will deal with them and instructed not to come back with any other more evil spirits to an empty house (the person with the spirit been casted out). A good time to ask the person in need of ministry, to invite the Holy Spirit (ruach ha-kodesh) into their lives again to prevent the spirit leaving, to come back with other evil spirits to an empty house (the person concerned). Mat 12:43 'When the unclean spirit has gone out of a man, he walks through dry places seeking rest, and finds none. :44 Then he said, I will return into my house from where I came out. And when he has come, he finds it empty, swept, and decorated. :45 Then he goes and takes with him seven other spirits more evil than himself, and they enter in and live there. And the last state of that man is worse than the first. Even so it also shall be to this evil generation.'
Here are some of the ways the evil spirit of pride manifests itself in a disguised form in us.

1.   Achievements of self and others.

How quickly can we hide behind past achievements? It could be records in sport or academics we held many years ago, probably broken over and over again and long forgotten. But it could be a way of boosting ourselves a little, especially to counter someone else talking about their achievements. Just to let people know that we are not the 'average Joe.' Some would even exaggerate (add a little white lie) to make their achievements sound higher and better than that of the other person. Sometimes we would subtly drop the fact that we were at University, or have this or that degree just to let people know 'who they are talking to'.

Psa 75:4 'I said to the proud, Do not boast; and to the wicked, Do not lift up the horn;.' Jas 4:16 'But now you boast in your presumptions. All such boasting is evil.'

2. Adopting another persona / image

Sometimes a person / people would deny who they are and take on another personality, or they might deny their race or culture. Lying and hiding their true identity. Too proud to acknowledge who they really are. It could be because of historical facts or that their race might be something that is mocked or looked down upon. To avoid this, they hide and pretend.

In South Africa the majority of people are throwing away their mother tongue (Zulu, Xhosa, Venda, Afrikaans etc.) pretending to be 'English speaking'. With it, their cultures also fly out the window because they are pretending to be somebody else. Not sure exactly what! Parents forsake family-names for their kids for fancy English names of actors and popstars. It could be funny and amusing at times. A sort of 'going back to the Tower of Babel' that we read about in Gen.11. It is clear that there are powerful forces working world-wide to pursue this agenda of 'oneness'. One world government, language, church, culture, economy, currency and the like. It will be easier for them to control the world this way. Some people are totally unaware of this, and simply follow and believe without questioning, reasoning and debating this phenomenon, thinking that they are now 'global citizens.'

3.   Adultery

Some men, and sometimes women just can't be faithful to their spouses. They have to steal someone else's glory. A wife is her husband's glory. It is nothing but pride to think that you as a married person deserve another or many other partners. It is outside God's laws and therefore breaking them makes you proud and rebellious. Exo 20:14 'Thou shalt not commit adultery.'
 We know that David committed adultery with Bathsheba. When David saw her, he desired her physically. When he found out that she was married, he sent her husband, with clear instructions to his general, to put Uriah (her husband) in front of the battlefield so that he can be killed. This happened as David planned. He also had intercourse with Bathsheba before Uriah died and made her pregnant. So much the more reason to have her husband killed. 2Sa 11:26 'And when the wife of Uriah heard that Uriah her husband was dead, she mourned for her husband. :27 And when the mourning was past, David sent and fetched her to his house, and she became his wife, and bare him a son. But the thing that David had done displeased the LORD.'
We also read in Gen. 16 that Abram's wife could not bear him a child. God promised Abram that his descendants would become a great nation. Abram became restless and could not wait. His wife was

barren and way past childbearing age. So, with Sarai (his wife) approval, Abram had a child with Hagar which was an Egyptian slave in his household. Their son, Ishmael is to this day the enemy of the son of the promise (Isaac). It appears that the descendants of Ishmael are the mainly Moslem nations. Isaacs's descendants are mainly people of the Judeo-Christian faith, and they not happy campers together. This was because we can't wait on God's promises. We need to help Him along because we get impatient (which is a sign of pride).

4. <u>Always late</u>

You get people who habitually arrive late for appointments. There are times in our lives where we don't have a choice, like traffic jams, flat tires etc. These are legitimate reasons. But when it is part of people's lifestyle, it makes them prideful. The attitude is: other people can wait for me. It makes me important; it makes me stand out from the crowd who is waiting for me. The person / people waiting for me might react negatively about me being inconsiderate, but that actually is a sign of how important I am. Friends stop making appointments or dates with people like this because they are unreliable. People like this develop a reputation of not being trustworthy or caring: Ecc 7:1a 'A good name is better than precious ointment…'
I believe there are things like Godly appointments. Could it be that people who are always late could miss these appointments?

5. Anger

Anger directed at evil-doing can be constructive. If one comes across a man raping somebody, anger is a natural reaction. If this anger goes over into righteous action, as it should, there can be nothing wrong with it. But when one develops a reputation for his anger / temper and people tiptoe around him, and his family obeys everything he says as to not make him angry, he uses that to always have his way, and so controls them. When Jesus cleaned the temple it was righteous anger because they were defiling the place of His Father with all kinds of trade and disrespect. Mat 21:12 'And Jesus went into the temple of God, and cast out all them that sold and bought in the temple, and overthrew the tables of the moneychangers, and the seats of them that sold doves.'

Paul does not deny the fact that we do get angry, but says we must deal with it and don't go and sleep on it. That is when it leads to bitterness and revenge and ultimately to nervous-breakdowns and even diseases. Eph 4:26 'Be ye angry, and sin not: let not the sun go down upon your wrath: 27 Neither give place to the devil.'

6. Being Argumentative

What an unpleasant experience being in the company of such a person. Always questioning what you say, and often tries to disprove you, just so they can win the argument. Their prideful egos satisfied that they won the day and is 'one up on you' because they believe they won and ended as the 'top dog'.

How has this spirit ruined relationships in business, causing church splits, marriage breakdowns, family splits and the list goes on.

1Ti 6:3 'If anyone teaches otherwise, and does not consent to wholesome words (those of our Lord Jesus Christ), and to the doctrine according to godliness, :4 he is proud, knowing nothing. He is sick concerning doubts and arguments, from which comes envy, strife, evil speakings, evil suspicions, :5 meddling, of men whose minds have been corrupted and deprived of the truth, supposing that gain is godliness. Withdraw from such.'

7.   Arrogance

Pro 8:13 'The fear of the LORD is to hate evil: pride, and arrogancy, and the evil way, and the froward mouth, do I hate.'

I shudder when I read that God' hates something. Hate is a very strong word. The word in the KJV 'arrogancy' is the same as arrogance. When we talk bad and down to, and about other people or races, we are nothing but arrogant. Arrogance is not limited to individuals but can be found in nations, governments, sport teams and organizations. Here are some quotes from the MKJV about being 'haughty' :

Pro 16:18 'Pride goes before destruction and a haughty spirit before a fall.'

Pro 21:24 'Proud, haughty scorner is his name, he who deals in proud wrath.'

Eze 16:50 'And they were haughty and did abominable things before Me, so I turned away as I saw fit.'

1Sa 2:3 'Talk no more so very proudly. Remove arrogance out of your mouth, for Jehovah is a God of knowledge, and by Him actions are weighed.'

Isa 13:11 'And I will visit evil on the world, and their iniquity on the wicked. And I will cause the arrogance of the proud to cease, and will lay low the pride of tyrants.'

8.   Atheism

Man wants to be his own god. Not wanting to answer to anybody. The captain of his own ship. One, who creates, designs and follows his own destiny. Therefore, he doesn't need a God. Atheists see this as being controlled by a being whom they believe doesn't exist. One of the chief proponents of aggressive atheism is scientist Richard Dawkins. He was heavily involved with a campaign in London where the following slogan was put on public buses. The slogan was: "There's probably no god. Now stop worrying and enjoy your life." Wonder why the word 'probably' is put in there? It certainly leaves the argument wide open and shows signs of uncertainty. Quite humorous if you think about it.

There is the case of Piltdown man. Here is a quote from Wikipedia about this case.

'The Piltdown Man was a paleoanthropological hoax in which bone fragments were presented as the fossilized remains of a previously unknown early human. These fragments consisted of parts of a skull and jawbone, said to have been collected in 1912 from a gravel pit at Piltdown, East Sussex, England. The Latin name *Eoanthropus dawsoni* ("Dawson's dawn-man", after the collector Charles Dawson) was given to the specimen. The significance of the specimen remained the subject of controversy until it was exposed in 1953 as a forgery, consisting of the lower jawbone of an orangutan deliberately combined with the cranium of a fully developed modern human.'

Many 'scientific' articles were published in all kinds of 'scientific' journals and apparently a few doctoral dissertations saw the light based on this 'scientific' evidence.
Scripture is clear about atheism. Psa 10:4 'Through the pride of his face the wicked will not seek Him; There is no God in all his schemes.'

Psa 53:1 'The fool has said in his heart, There is no God. They acted corruptly, and have worked out abominable wickedness; there is not one doing good.'

9. Center of attention

How the enemy can try to make us feel important. Some people will do everything to be the center of attention. When in a conversation with other people they will try and capture and keep the attention of the one speaking as if they are the only person in the conversation. They will try their utmost to keep the conversation directed towards them, constantly interrupting the person speaking with questions to keep his / her attention. At parties you will always find one, or maybe more

competing, to be the 'belle of the ball'. The whole party should be focused on them. When they can't achieve this, the party, according to them, was a failure. Although they know this attention is fleeting and often false, they still need it to stroke their ego, and really can't help themselves.
Joh 5:44 'How can you believe, you who receive honor from one another and do not seek the honor that comes from God only?'
1Th 2:6 'Nor did we seek glory from men, neither from you nor from others, being able to be so with heaviness, as apostles of Christ.'

10. Claiming God's and other people's credit

You would find people who would quote and repeat what someone said as if they were the first to say or discovered this truth. Often forgetting or ignoring that you were in the very conversation where you heard someone else say something or explaining a discovery they made. It could be something the pastor said in his sermon, but this person would claim the honor and credit and make it sound as if it was their clever research and insight that brought this fact to light.
How often something happens in our lives which blessed us, and we claim that it was some circumstance or some effort of our own that brought it along.
When people tried to build a tower to the heavens, God wasn't very impressed by this. In Genesis 11 we read about this story:
Gen 11:2 'And it came to pass, as they journeyed from the east, that they found a plain in the land of Shinar; and they dwelt there. : 3 And they said one

to another, Go to, let us make brick, and burn them thoroughly. And they had brick for stone, and slime had they for mortar. :4 And they said, Go to, let us build us a city and a tower, whose top may reach unto heaven; and let us make us a name, lest we be scattered abroad upon the face of the whole earth. :5 And the LORD came down to see the city and the tower, which the children of men builded. :6 And the LORD said, Behold, the people is one, and they have all one language; and this they begin to do: and now nothing will be restrained from them, which they have imagined to do. : 7 Go to, let us go down, and there confound their language, that they may not understand one another's speech. : 8 So the LORD scattered them abroad from thence upon the face of all the earth: and they left off to build the city.
: 9 Therefore is the name of it called Babel; because the LORD did there confound the language of all the earth: and from thence did the LORD scatter them abroad upon the face of all the earth.'

In Daniel we read about the pride and self-exaltation of King Nebuchadnezzar. Praising himself and 'his' achievements. The results weren't good.

Dan 4:30 'The king spake, and said, Is not this great Babylon, that I have built for the house of the kingdom by the might of my power, and for the honour of my majesty? :31 While the word was in the king's mouth, there fell a voice from heaven, saying, O king Nebuchadnezzar, to thee it is spoken; The kingdom is departed from thee. :32 And they shall drive thee from men, and thy dwelling shall be with the beasts of the field: they

shall make thee to eat grass as oxen, and seven times shall pass over thee, until thou know that the most High ruleth in the kingdom of men, and giveth it to whomsoever he will.'
Indeed, he spent some time out in the field eating grass like an animal.
How often would we hear about someone that was healed of a disease, someone we knew and prayed for, and then keep on boasting to people how our prayers healed them? As if it only depended on our prayers, leaving God totally out of the picture. Let's be beware of eating grass and stealing God's glory. God does not share it.

11. Comparisons and competition

How we like to compare ourselves, especially with those weaker and lower than us. That way we can elevate ourselves. We have 'legitimate' grounds to look down on them. The 'facts' proof that we are better, or on a higher level than them. This even functions on a spiritual level. People who don't know as much about a spiritual/ biblical subject are frowned upon. Never mind the fact when we encounter someone who knows far more than us about a subject, we don't expect them to look down on us. Remember the Pharisee in the temple comparing himself with the tax-collector? Luk 18:9 'And he spake this parable unto certain which trusted in themselves that they were righteous, and despised others: :10 Two men went up into the temple to pray; the one a Pharisee, and the other a publican. :11 The Pharisee stood and prayed thus with himself, God, I thank thee, that I am not as other men are, extortioners, unjust, adulterers, or even as this publican. : 12 I fast twice in the week, I give tithes of all that I possess. :13 And the publican, standing afar off, would not lift up so much as his eyes unto heaven, but smote upon his breast, saying, God be merciful to me a sinner. :14 I tell you, this man went down to his house justified rather than the other: for every one that exalteth himself shall be abased; and he that humbleth himself shall be exalted.'

If someone talks about an achievement and we get a sense that he is boasting, and we feel that we have achieved better and higher in that area, we would quickly mention it to cut them down to size and tell them of 'our' achievements, and if we haven't really made waves in that area, we would mention a family member or acquaintance who have achieved better than this person. In that way we feel we bring him / them down to the level they need to be. 'Cut them down to size.'
Paul says we shouldn't think of ourselves more highly than others: Rom 12:3 'For I say, through the grace given unto me, to every man that is among you, not to think of himself more highly than he ought to think; but to think soberly, according as God hath dealt to every man the measure of faith.'

12. Unable to give compliments

I often had the urge to give someone an honest compliment for various reasons, but when I tried to, I found that the words would not come. A few times I managed to 'break through' and actually do it, and then felt embarrassed and shy about it. I

could not understand this, but today I understand it as nothing but pride. Somehow, we feel it will elevate the person too much and might give them a 'big head' if we humble ourselves and ask for forgiveness. We don't want them to feel too important and think too much of themselves. We are fearful of elevating people. You also find people who easily compliment people but, in your heart, you feel and know they don't mean it. Sometimes we use it to manipulate people with these compliments while we have a secret agenda and want something from them.
Php 2:3 'Let nothing be done through strife or vainglory, but in lowliness of mind let each esteem others better than themselves.'

13.　　Control, manipulation and power

Very few people seem to have the capacity to withstand this evil spirit. How easily do we invite this spirit in to control us, so we can control others? Our desire to control everything is usually seated in hurt. We build tight scales, like leviathan around that hurt so that no air or light can come in. Nobody is allowed close to it. When they dare, we snap at them with leviathan-like jaws and teeth. Stay away, I won't get hurt again! is what we try to say.
This spirit is the most divisive spirit there is. It operates in marriages, families, churches and business. It does not discriminate against race, gender or age.
I have found that quilt is often used as a very effective tool in accomplishing this control. How often would parents, usually aging ones with adult children use this weapon against their kids? They

might feel lonely while their children are trying to get on with their own lives. They feel neglected, especially if they are single because they are divorced or their spouse died. The common method is asking the 'Why' question. Why didn't you phone me – why didn't you do this or that? This way they invoke quilt in their children, and now they can control them. When the kids were younger and living at home, it was easier to control them because they were dependent on their parents. Parents could control them by withholding pocket money, not allowing them to go places or attend certain events, even threatening and spanking them as a way of keeping them in check. I don't believe that all this is wrong if kids constantly disobey their parents. Parents should explain to them that it is a way of disciplining them. That there are rules and that nobody can just do what he likes. Every game has rules and often a referee. You play outside the rules, the whistle blows and there is a penalty against you or your team.

Off course you have children controlling their parents with tears and tantrums. You have the wife who controls and manipulates the husband or kids with tears. A husband or father who controls with threats and violence. Married couples who threaten each other with divorce or having extra marital affairs as a way of control if the other doesn't want to dance to their tunes.

Then there is the silent / dumb stupor trick. The one who believes an offence was committed against them, goes and hide in their cave. Doesn't talk at all, or as little as possible. The 'guilty ones' must now wonder what they have done wrong. When questioned about this hiding, the answers are often vague and evasive. I want you to feel guilty and suffer and wrestle with what you possibly did wrong. Keep on guessing, and when you hit the right key, then I will slowly forgive you if you stay on your knees long enough.

Controlling is what we like to do to others, but we can't stand it when people do it to us.

The well-known story in the bible about Jezebel is a fine example of control and how the Jezebel spirit works. The story is about her husband, Ahab, who wanted to buy Naboth's vineyard, but it was not for sale. Ahab's reaction was to withdraw himself by sulking. His wicked wife Jezebel, who was an idolatrous Baal worshipper and deeply into witchcraft, enquired about his little tantrum, and he told her about Naboth who refused to sell his vineyard to him. Jezebel seized the opportunity to take control, taking over her husband's role. The Jezebel spirit in a person is constantly looking for opportunities like this. She arranged that Naboth be killed (The same as David did with Uriah who was standing between him and Bathsheba) in order that her husband can get Naboth's vineyard. In God's order, the husband is Priest, Prophet and King in his household. Not to lord it over, but to guide, show the direction and lead the way. Make decisions with his wife, but at the end take responsibility for it. Not the blaming game that Adam did trying to blame it on his wife, while he was fully aware of what was going on. If this order is disturbed by the Jezebel spirit of control, things go horribly wrong.

They became a wicked pair, and Elijah the prophet predicted that the dogs will feast on the remains of her body. It happened exactly like that.

Jezebel recognizes her husband's sadness:

1Ki 21:5 'But Jezebel his wife came to him, and said unto him, Why is thy spirit so sad, that thou eatest no bread?'

1Ki 21:7 'And Jezebel his wife said unto him, Dost thou now govern the kingdom of Israel? arise, and eat bread, and let thine heart be merry: I will give thee the vineyard of Naboth the Jezreelite.'

Jezebel has Naboth killed:

Ki 21:15 'And it came to pass, when Jezebel heard that Naboth was stoned, and was dead, that Jezebel said to Ahab, Arise, take possession of the vineyard of Naboth the Jezreelite, which he refused to give thee for money: for Naboth is not alive, but dead.'

Jezebel takes control of her husband, King Ahab's affairs:

1Ki 21:8 'So she wrote letters in Ahab's name, and sealed them with his seal, and sent the letters unto the elders and to the nobles that were in his city, dwelling with Naboth.'

Elijah predicted her death.
1Ki 21:23 'And of Jezebel also spake the LORD, saying, The dogs shall eat Jezebel by the wall of Jezreel.'

Jezebel knew about her fate and demise. When Jehu came to kill her, she first went and made up her face. What vanity! And then her death.

2Ki 9:30 'And when Jehu was come to Jezreel, Jezebel heard of it; and she painted her face, and tired her head, and looked out at a window. :31 And as Jehu entered in at the gate, she said, Had

Zimri peace, who slew his master? :32 And he lifted up his face to the window, and said, Who is on my side? who? And there looked out to him two or three eunuchs. :33 And he said, Throw her down. So they threw her down: and some of her blood was sprinkled on the wall, and on the horses: and he trode her under foot. :34 And when he was come in, he did eat and drink, and said, Go, see now this cursed woman, and bury her: for she is a king's daughter. 9:35 And they went to bury her: but they found no more of her than the skull, and the feet, and the palms of her hands. :36 Wherefore they came again, and told him. And he said, This is the word of the LORD, which he spake by his servant Elijah the Tishbite, saying, In the portion of Jezreel shall dogs eat the flesh of Jezebel: :37 And the carcase of Jezebel shall be as dung upon the face of the field in the portion of Jezreel; so that they shall not say, This is Jezebel.'
That is what controlling can lead to, death and murder. People can be so frustrated by the fact that they can't control someone, that they actually murder them. Usually, it leads to death in areas or relationships, progress in one's financial or spiritual life. Yes, we even try to control God sometimes. God, I want this or that and I want it now. Sometimes God grants our wishes quickly, other times we have to wait, and other times the answer is NO! That, we have to accept, but the controlling spirit in us will constantly remind us of God's injustice and unfairness. I have a brother who is mentally impaired. He can talk, wash himself (to an extent), make himself coffee or tea and something basic to eat. It is absolutely amazing how he can invoke this controlling spirit in people. When he walks into a gathering of family

members, one can literally see some (usually the same crowd) physically reacting. They would immediately start giving him commands to sit, stand or do something. Feeling the need to control him somehow. It is as if this controlling Jezebel spirit can sense spirits that are 'weaker' and immediately gives the command to take control and manipulate it.

14.   Critical spirit

How critical can we be of everything? I know a couple where the wife is a 'go getter'. More than often, reckless. Always scheming of ways of doing business and making money. Seldom considering risks, or doing a business plan. Her husband, probably also because he has suffered under some of her wild attempts of making money, is the exact opposite. He analyzes every plan she comes up with into oblivion. His critical spirit drives him until he can see no chance of it succeeding. While other people also saw the opportunity, made their analysis and decision, took the bull by the horns and were making money, he is still hard at work proofing (through circular and repetitive analyzes) that it can't work. Usually, people with a critical spirit can be very judgmental, although scripture clearly warn us against it. Jesus said: Mat 7:1 'Judge not, that you may not be judged. :2 For with whatever judgment you judge, you shall be judged; and with whatever measure you measure out, it shall be measured to you again. :3 And why do you look on the splinter that is in your brother's eye, but do not consider the beam that is in your own eye? :4 Or how will you say to your brother, Let me pull the splinter out of your eye; and, behold, a beam is in your own eye?

:5 Hypocrite! First cast the beam out of your own eye, and then you shall see clearly to cast the splinter out of your brother's eye.'

I have heard witnesses where people tell how they experienced the glorious presence of God in a group, and then one person says something critical about another movement or church of God, and the glory would disappear immediately. God does not look favourably on this spirit operating in us.

Then there is this beautiful story in John 8 where the Pharisees brought a woman to Jesus caught red-handed in Adultery. This is how Jesus dealt with this critical / judgmental spirit: Joh 8:3 'And the scribes and Pharisees brought to Him a woman taken in adultery. And standing her in the midst, :4 they said to Him, Teacher, this woman was taken in adultery, in the very act. :5 Now Moses in the Law commanded us that such should be stoned. You, then, what do you say? :6 They said this, tempting Him so that they might have reason to accuse Him. But bending down, Jesus wrote on the ground with His finger, not appearing to hear. :7 But as they continued to ask Him, He lifted Himself up and said to them, He who is without sin among you, let him cast the first stone at her. :8 And again bending down, He wrote on the ground. :9 And hearing, and being convicted by conscience, they went out one by one, beginning at the oldest, until the last. And Jesus was left alone, and the woman standing in the midst. :10 And bending back up, and seeing no one but the woman, Jesus said to her, Woman, where are the ones who accused you? Did not one give judgment against you? :11 And she said, No one, Lord. And Jesus said to her, Neither do I give judgment. Go, and sin no more.'

Somebody once said that the 'Christian' army is the only one that shoots its wounded. How mightily fellow Christians can come down on their fallen brothers and sisters instead of helping them up, supporting and covering them with prayers. How lonely and isolated the fallen must feel, and on top of this, the barrage of damnation, accusations and finger-pointing from those who must comfort and support them. There is nothing wrong in reprimanding someone about sin, but it must always be accompanied by pointing out that after they confessed, that Christ has forgiven them, and that they must go make right if they sinned against a person, so relationships can be restored and they are set free and don't have to walk around with guilt. Also important, they must forgive themselves. We sometimes confess, repent, ask for forgiveness, but then walk around with something gnawing feeling that the problem is not resolved. It is because they haven't forgiven themselves.

15. The desire for power and riches

How I slaved away to become 'financially independent', a sort of self-styled / self-made millionaire. Whilst having a fulltime job, I always had something going on as a sideline. Trying various things, often burning my fingers. I wore myself out, just keeping head above water. My dream was to make enough money, and then buy a cottage by the sea where I can write full-time. As

one get older you realize that moment would hardly ever come, because once you have money, you always want more. Always scared that what you have is not enough. I believe God wants us to work hard and be honest; the only problem is we believe the outcome depends solely on ourselves. Having money is not a sin. It is a blessing from God, but it is the *love* of money that is the problem. Here is what Paul and scripture says about money: 1Ti 6:10 'For the love of money is a root of all evils, of which some having lusted after, they were seduced from the faith and pierced themselves through with many sorrows.'
Heb 13:5 'Let your way of life be without the love of money, and be content with such things as you have, for He has said, "Not at all will I leave you, not at all will I forsake you, never!.'
Often our hard work is focused on making us wealthier than our brother / neighbour so we can show of the latest 'gadgets' we bought. This 'keeping up with the Joneses' can really tire, and make us envious, leading to stress and burnout.

16. <u>Disloyalty</u>

How disloyal we can be to spouses, family, or employers etc. Coming late for work with poor excuses. Not honouring our appointments with our spouses or children, often when they need us the most. Not attending some important meetings and functions at work because we have a grudge against our boss or a co-worker and missing out on bonding and team-building with our fellow workers. Missing out on opportunities to 'be there' for our spouse or kids when they might really need us. Worse of all, being disloyal towards God by throwing his precepts and principals down the drain. Doing our 'own' thing 'our' way. A fine example in the Bible was David's loyalty towards Saul. Saul even tried to kill David.1Sa 18:10 'And it happened on the next day the evil spirit from God came on Saul, and he prophesied in the midst of the house. And David played with his hand, as at other times. And a spear was in Saul's hand.:11 And Saul threw the spear. For he said, I will strike David even to the wall. And David drew back out of his presence twice.'

David's loyalty towards Saul was because he believed that Saul was anointed by Samuel, who was ordered by God to do so. David had opportunities to kill Saul, but refused because of this loyalty towards him: 1Sa 26:7 'So David and Abishai came to the people by night. And behold, Saul lay sleeping in the tent, and his spear stuck in the ground at his head. But Abner and the people lay around him. :8 And Abishai said to David, God has shut up your enemy into your hand this day. And please let me strike him with the spear even to the earth at once, and I will not repeat it to him.:9 And David said to Abishai, Do not destroy him. For who can stretch forth his hand against Jehovah's anointed and be guiltless?'

17. Division / Denominations / Divorce

A telltale sign of Satan's presence, is division. His strategy is 'divide and rule'. Whenever you come across this phenomenon, you now know who is behind it. This divisive spirit is behind divorce, business breakups, and it's especially active in churches. Two business partners (often both Christian) all of a sudden argue about minor things, accusing each other of all kinds of misdeeds. Two pastors having arguments over dogmas or interpretation of some scripture, or minuscule things on church-growth or some building alterations. In marriage one partner will constantly find fault with the other one. Partners accusing each other falsely. The list goes on. Satan is the accuser of the brethren: Rev 12:10 'And I heard a loud voice saying in heaven, Now is come salvation, and strength, and the kingdom of our God, and the power of his Christ: for the accuser of our brethren is cast down, which accused them before our God day and night.' Often churches, business and marriage's split up with great bitterness and loss to both parties (emotionally and financially scarred) and Satan is laughing all the way. Yes, I know. I have been down that road. And so, the Christian church, so called Christian business partnerships and Christian marriages becomes the laughing stock of the world. The secular world now has ample ammunition to shoot at Christianity, pointing out that it simply isn't worth following Christ. How many 'Christian' denominations are there today? - thousands, and still counting, all because of this spirit. The apostle Paul calls for unity in the church, very well aware of this divisive spirit working in the early church already: 1Co 1:10 'Now I beseech you, brethren, by the name of our Lord Jesus Christ, that ye all speak the same thing, and that there be no divisions among you; but that ye be perfectly joined together in the same mind and in the same judgment.'

The Greek word Paul is using here for 'divisions' is 'schisma'. Here is the Strong's definition:

    σχίσμα

schisma

skhis'-mah

From G4977; a *split* or *gap* ("schism"), literally or figuratively: - division, rent, schism. This is where the English word 'schism' comes from.
In the Cambridge advanced learners Dictionary is this definition: '**schism** /ˈskɪz.əm/ , /ˈsɪz-/ *noun* [C] a division into two groups caused by a disagreement about ideas, especially in a religious organization - *a schism **in/within** the Church.*'

Interesting that in the dictionary, it uses the church as an example!
In Paul's letter to the Ephesians he pleads for this unity. Take note of verse 4:3 where the talks about the 'unity of the Spirit...'
Eph 4:1 'I therefore, the prisoner of the Lord, beseech you that ye walk worthy of the vocation wherewith ye are called, :2 With all lowliness and meekness, with longsuffering, forbearing one another in love; :3 Endeavoring to keep the unity of the Spirit in the bond of peace. :4 There is one body, and one Spirit, even as ye are called in one hope of your calling; :5 One Lord, one faith, one baptism, :6 One God and Father of all, who is above all, and through all, and in you all.'

18 Envy / Jealousy and Strife

How we envy what others have? Material things, abilities and others position of power and prestige. Envy can bring a rift in relationships. Trying to get even with them because they have things we want and desire. Envy makes us jealous. Angry about what we don't have. This leads to bitterness. Scripture is clear about the effects of this spirit that can occupy us.

Pro 14:30 'A sound heart is the life of the flesh: but envy the rottenness of the bones.'

I suffer from 'gout' at times. It is inflammation that causes pain in the joints. Maybe a 'rottenness of the bones'?

In Romans Paul talks about envy in the same light as other vile sins such as murder etc. Rom 1:29 'Being filled with all unighteousness, fornication, wickedness, covetousness, maliciousness; full of envy, murder, debate, deceit, malignity; whisperers,'

James says that envy leads to all kind of confusion: Jas 3:16 'For where envying and strife is, there is confusion and every evil work.'

According to the bible Jesus was also captured and handed over to Pilate because of envy: Mat 27:17 'Therefore when they were gathered together, Pilate said unto them, Whom will ye that I release unto you? Barabbas or Jesus which is called Christ? :18 For he knew that for envy they had delivered him.'

Yes, these are all things that lead to all kinds of evil. In the Song of Solomon, we read about jealousy: Son 8:6 'Set me as a seal upon thine heart, as a seal upon thine arm: for love is strong as death; jealousy is cruel as the grave: the coals thereof are coals of fire, which hath a most vehement flame.'

Envy always leads to strife. James says the following:

Jas 3:14 'But if ye have bitter envying and strife in your hearts, glory not, and lie not against the truth. :15 This wisdom descendeth not from above, but is earthly, sensual, devilish.'

Jacob loved his son Joseph more that his other children. The siblings hated Joseph for this. Then Joseph had a dream in which he saw his brothers bowing down to him. This enraged them and increased their hate for him: Gen 37:3 'And Israel loved Joseph more than all his sons, because he was the son of his old age. And he made him a tunic reaching to the soles of his feet. :4 And when his brothers saw that their father loved him more than all his brothers, they hated him, and could not speak peaceably to him.: 5 And Joseph dreamed a dream and told it to his brothers. And they hated him still more. :6 And he said to them, I pray you, Hear this dream which I have dreamed. :7 For behold! We were binding sheaves in the middle of the field, and lo, my sheaf arose and also stood upright. And behold, your sheaves stood around and bowed down to my sheaf. :8 And his brothers said to him, Shall you indeed reign over us? Or shall you indeed have the rule over us? And they hated him still more for his dreams and for his words.'

We know further in the story that Jacob sent Joseph to his brothers who was away tending the flock. When Joseph reached them, they considered killing him, but the one brother objected and they stripped of the coat Jacob made for him, threw him in a pit, and eventually sold him into slavery. That is what jealousy does to people.

In this case, brothers contemplating killing another brother.

19. <u>Fear and worry</u>

How often can these two factors either drive us or leave us hopeless, lame and indecisive. Some people use it to be driven. Always restless. Must achieve more, working day and night to accumulate and heap up. Always scared that they will run into lack. Often getting to the end of their lives and regretting that they didn't take more time off to relax and spent time with their families. Sometimes their children, now grown up, are total strangers to them.
This is what Christ taught about worry: Mat 6:25 'Therefore I say to you, Do not be anxious for your life, what you shall eat, or what you shall drink; nor for your body, what you shall put on. Is not life more than food and the body more than clothing? :26 Behold the birds of the air; for they sow not, nor do they reap, nor gather into barns. Yet your heavenly Father feeds them; are you not much better than they are?
:27 Which of you by being anxious can add one cubit to his stature? :28 And why are you anxious about clothing? Consider the lilies of the field, how they grow. They do not toil, nor do they spin, :29 but I say to you that even Solomon in his glory was not arrayed like one of these. :30 Therefore if God so clothes the grass of the field, which today is, and tomorrow is thrown into the oven, will He not much rather clothe you, little-faiths? :31 Therefore do not be anxious, saying, What shall we eat? or, What shall we drink? or, With what shall we be clothed? :32 For the nations seek after

all these things. For your heavenly Father knows that you have need of all these things. :33 But seek first the kingdom of God and His righteousness; and all these things shall be added to you.'

Maybe we ignore this command by Christ, because it (food, clothes etc.) will be given *after* we 'first seek the kingdom of God'. That seems like a daunting task, and it is easier to follow our own route and tolerate the fear and worry about what tomorrow will bring.

Peter says: 1Pe 5:6 'Humble yourselves therefore under the mighty hand of God, that he may exalt you in due time: :7 Casting all your care upon him; for he careth for you.'
All our worries and fears should be cast upon Jesus. He cares for us and knows and understands our troubles.

Isaiah tells us why we shouldn't fear: Isa 41:13 'For I the LORD thy God will hold thy right hand, saying unto thee, Fear not; I will help thee.'

Some people have a fear at times to give their opinion because they might be wrong and even reprimanded. That can be too much for their egos.

Fears are also called 'Phobias' in the academic world. If you look on Wikipedia on the internet, you find there are over 150 identified phobias (fears) people have. Phobias of heaven, cheese, religion, all kinds of animals, even a fear of Christians, technology and on and on, while Jesus says we shouldn't worry about these things.

20. Gossip

How easy is it for this evil to become our favourite pastime? Sitting idly around a teapot and 'discussing' some matters. Usually talking about a person, a group or a colleague, more than often, just speculating and second guessing about a peculiarity or problem that someone has. Something they have done, good or bad, and then discussing the effect of their actions and possible answers or punishment that is needed. Satan even uses us at prayer-meetings where someone would very seriously mention that 'we must really pray for so and so' and then when asked 'pray for what'? then they will come out with the hidden piece of gossip: I 'hear' so and so are getting divorced. Often based on 'hear say'. Everything nicely disguised as 'Christian concern' for the other party. What a lie! How often do people hear something about another person and then tell others about it, adding a little tail to it, and so more and more people add some news, and eventually it becomes a very ugly situation breaking up relationships, and the Enemy laughs. The bible has a lot to say about the effect of our words and how we should guard our tongue.

Eph 4:29 'Let no corrupt communication proceed out of your mouth, but that which is good to the use of edifying, that it may minister grace unto the hearers.'

Here are particular condemning words by Jesus himself of how we should think before we speak carelessly: Mat 12:36 'But I say unto you, That every idle word that men shall speak, they shall give account thereof in the day of judgment.'

The bible often refers to gossipers as 'whisperers' /'talebearer' or a 'tattler'. The MJKV says this about a whisperer:
Pro 16:28 'A perverse man causes fighting and a whisperer separates chief friends.'
1Ti 5:13 'And withal they learn to be idle, wandering about from house to house; and not only idle, but tattlers also and busybodies, speaking things which they ought not.' In other translations, tattlers are mentioned as 'gossips'
Paul equates whisperers to things like murder:
Rom 1:29 'Being filled with all unrighteousness, fornication, wickedness, covetousness, maliciousness; full of envy, murder, debate, deceit, malignity; whisperers.'
In Proverbs it is suggested that gossip and lying can make people sick:
Pro 18:8 'The words of a talebearer are as wounds, and they go down into the innermost parts of the belly.'

James also says that an untamed tongue is poison and that we should be careful with words. Not idly sit around and gossip without thinking of the implications of our words. Jas 3:1 'My brethren, be not many masters, knowing that we shall receive the greater condemnation. :2 For in many things we offend all. If any man offend not in word, the same is a perfect man, and able also to bridle the whole body. :3 Behold, we put bits in the horses' mouths, that they may obey us; and we turn about their whole body. :4 Behold also the ships, which though they be so great, and are driven of fierce winds, yet are they turned about with a very small helm, whithersoever the governor listeth. :5 Even so the tongue is a little member, and boasteth great things. Behold how great a matter a little fire kindleth! :6 And the tongue is a fire, a world of iniquity: so is the tongue among our members, that it defileth the whole body, and setteth on fire the course of nature; and it is set on fire of hell. :7 For every kind of beasts, and of birds, and of serpents, and of things in the sea, is tamed, and hath been tamed of mankind: :8 But the tongue can no man tame; it is an unruly evil, full of deadly poison.'

21. <u>Humour and Sarcasm</u>

Many people complemented me on my 'wit' and how sharp I was with words. Most found my dark humour very funny. One day a friend phoned me and started sharing his hurt with me about a love affair that went sour. It wasn't long and I was trying to turn it into something humorous. I could identify with his hurt, but did not know how to handle the situation. I was trying to avoid talking about the situation because I didn't know how to deal with my own hurt. He asked me (rather annoyed) why do I always shy away from these emotional conversations and try and make a joke of it. He nailed me there. It was the first time somebody was this honest with me. Deep inside I knew I was doing it, but thought 'that is just the way I am'. From then on, it worried me, but still didn't deal with it because I didn't know how.
It was much later, and possibly many victims of my 'wit' and so called 'humour' later, that I realized that it was just wicked pride. I was trying to avoid these emotional talks because it was 'to close to home'. The longer I listened to people pouring their heart and sorrow out, the more painful it was

to me. How can one deal with issues that you haven't sorted out in your own heart? A humble heart is one that can listen to someone's problems even if you haven't had the experiences they had. Not always trying to give advice, but just be there as a 'shoulder to cry on'. More than often, that is what the grieving person wants. How often do we stop telling people about our deepest hurt because often you not even half-way, and they have a quick solution? The person is just trying to get you of their back and end, or divert the conversation. After speaking to a few people about the issue, you have more quick solutions than you had listeners.

Pride is trying to protect us. Pride is telling us to deny the fact that we are hurting ourselves, and that we are unable to deal with it.

Humour and sarcasm are often used to tell people, in a very undercover way, how silly or stupid they are. This usually happens in the presence of other people and the 'victim' is laughed at and feels like an idiot.

Someone asked my father one day what he thought humour was. My dad answered: 'when you can make a joke at your own expense'. In other words, the joke is on yourself, and not somebody else.

When we use sarcasm and humour to hide something, we are not honest, and therefore lying. We are not helping the other person, or ourselves. When we hide something, we are practicing 'occult' (to hide something). We know that is the way Satan operates. He comes disguised, hiding, not showing his ugly face.

22. Idolatry

In Leviticus God clearly states that He does not like any form of idolatry: Lev 19:4 'Turn ye not unto idols, nor make to yourselves molten gods: I am the LORD your God.'

Lev 26:1 'Ye shall make you no idols nor graven image, neither rear you up a standing image, neither shall ye set up any image of stone in your land, to bow down unto it: for I am the LORD your God.'

In the Ten Commandments, God says the following: Exo 20:3 'Thou shalt have no other gods before me :4 Thou shalt not make unto thee any graven image, or any likeness of any thing that is in heaven above, or that is in the earth beneath, or that is in the water under the earth: :5 Thou shalt not bow down thyself to them, nor serve them: for I the LORD thy God am a jealous God, visiting the iniquity of the fathers upon the children unto the third and fourth generation of them that hate me; :6 And shewing mercy unto thousands of them that love me, and keep my commandments.'

How quickly can we run to 'other gods' when we don't get an instant answer from God. In this modern age of instant coffee, noodles and take away foods, we want everything NOW! If God doesn't give it to me now, I look toward other avenues for answers and help. Like the Israelites in the desert when Moses wasn't there as an intermediate between them and God, they decided to make an idol as their God.

Exo 32:1 'And the people saw that Moses delayed to come down from the mountain, and the people gathered themselves to Aaron. And they said to him, Up! Make us gods who shall go before us. For this Moses, the man who brought us up out of the land of Egypt, we do not know what has become of him. :2 'And Aaron said to them, break off the golden earrings which are in the ears of your wives, of your sons, and of your daughters, and bring them to me. :3 And all the people broke off the golden earrings which were in their ears, and brought them to Aaron. :4 And he took them from their hand, and fashioned it with an engraving tool. And he made it a molten calf. And they said, these are your gods, O Israel, who brought you up out of the land of Egypt.'

We read in 1Kings 18 how God, through the prophet Elijah dealt with the priests of Baal during the reign of King Ahab and his wicked wife Jezebel, because God hates false gods. When Saul didn't get an immediate answer from God, he went to a medium for answers. This did not please God. 1Sa 28:4 'And the Philistines gathered themselves and came and pitched in Shunem. And Saul gathered all Israel and they pitched in Gilboa. :5 And Saul saw the army of the Philistines, and he was afraid, and his heart greatly trembled. :6 And when Saul inquired of Jehovah, Jehovah did not answer him, neither by dreams, nor by Urim, nor by prophets. :7 And Saul said to his servants, Seek me a woman who is a medium, so that I may go to her and inquire of her. And his servant said to him, Behold, there is a woman who is a medium, at Endor.'

The medium of Endor called up the spirit of Samuel and this is what God's prophet told Saul: 1Sa 28:18 'Because you did not obey the voice of Jehovah, nor execute his fierce wrath on Amalek, therefore Jehovah has done this thing to you now. :19 And, Jehovah will also deliver Israel with you into the hand of the Philistines. And tomorrow you and your sons shall be with me. Jehovah also shall deliver the army of Israel into the hand of the Philistines. :20 And Saul immediately fell headlong on the earth, and was sorely afraid because of the words of Samuel. And there was no strength in him, for he had eaten no bread all day nor all night.'

Today Idolatry has become open mockery. There are programs on TV, which I think originated in America called 'Idols'. Here all kinds of musicians and artist are turned in idols. This has now spread and been copy-catted all over the world. Nearly every country with TV's has got and 'Idols' program. We will have to train ourselves patience to wait on God and not fall into idolatry because of our impatience. Our short-cuts will lead us down thorny paths, with results that we might regret like Saul did. Our Idolatry might not result in physical death, but there might be assaults on our finances, marriage, health or relationships. The enemy (Satan) will have legal ground to come in and steal and destroy.

23.   Impatience and irritability

We have seen that impatience leads to quick decisions and leading us away from God's plan. I once read about a man who made this confession where God gave him great insight into his own impatience and irritability. He tells of a colleague at work that really got on his nerves. The profanities, cursing and blasphemy of the guy was driving him up against the wall. The more he prayed for this person, the more impatient and irritated he became with this person. 'Why doesn't my prayers work, in fact, this guy is getting worse'. One day while struggling with God in prayer, he heard God drop this message in his heart. 'Why do want this colleague converted'. He could not believe his ears. Slowly God revealed to him that it was about himself, and not about the other guy. He only really wanted this guy converted to make things easier for himself at work. Caring more about his own discomfort with this guy at work, rather than his real conversation. What a revelation. How subtle can the enemy be? We have seen where this spirit of impatience has led many a men astray. The Israelites in the desert who got impatience because Moses stayed away too long, and convinced his brother Aaron, to make them an idol in the form of a calf that they can worship. Saul getting impatient with waiting for a message from the Lord and consulting a medium. In 2 Timothy Paul writes to Timothy about his own persecutions, endurance and patience: 2Ti 3:10 'But you have fully known my doctrine, manner of life, purpose, faith, long-suffering, love, patience, :11 persecutions, afflictions, such as happened to me at Antioch, at Iconium, at Lystra. What persecutions I endured! But the Lord delivered me out of all.'

We often forget the principle in the Bible of 'sowing and reaping'. A seed doesn't become a fruit-producing tree overnight. First the seed, then the roots, then the stem, then the flower / fruit. Farmers understand this process because they work with it every day. So, they have to wait for seasons and rain. James knew this.

Jas 5:7 'Therefore be patient, brothers, until the coming of the Lord. Behold, the farmer waits for the precious fruit of the earth and has long patience for it, until he receives the early and the latter rain. :8 You also be patient, establish your hearts, for the coming of your Lord draws near.' And so, there are many verses that call us to patience: Paul says it is the fruit of the Spirit: Gal 5:22 'But the fruit of the Spirit is love, joy, peace, longsuffering, gentleness, goodness, faith, :23 Meekness, temperance: against such there is no law.' Longsuffering means patience. Paul gives us further promises about patience: Col 1:11 'Strengthened with all might, according to his glorious power, unto all patience and longsuffering with joyfulness; :12 Giving thanks unto the Father, which hath made us meet to be partakers of the inheritance of the saints in light: :13 Who hath delivered us from the power of darkness, and hath translated us into the kingdom of his dear Son.' Isaiah promises great strength and physical well-being for those who are prepared to wait on the Lord.

Isa 40:31 'But they that wait upon the LORD shall renew their strength; they shall mount up with wings as eagles; they shall run, and not be weary; and they shall walk, and not faint.'

Psa 27:14 'Wait on the LORD: be of good courage, and he shall strengthen thine heart: wait, I say, on the LORD.'

In Ephesians Paul pleads for Unity that can only come through, inter alia, patience.

Eph 4:2 'With all lowliness and meekness, with longsuffering, forbearing one another in love; :3 Endeavoring to keep the unity of the Spirit in the bond of peace.'

24. Judgement

Judging others can come so quick and easy. It works along with the critical spirit. The critical spirit convinces us to judge. When we judge, we place ourselves in a higher position than the other person. We stand on the number 1 spot on the podium. We receive the trophy of righteousness. The other person/s are not on our level. We can look down on them from our elevated position. Scripture is very clear that there is, and in the last days, there will only be one judge and that is God himself. We are clearly demanded not to judge. Reprimanding a fellow Christian in love, is not judgement, but helping them.
Psa 7:8 'The LORD shall judge the people: judge me, O LORD, according to my righteousness, and according to mine integrity that is in me.'
Psa 75:7 'But God is the judge: he putteth down one, and setteth up another.'
Jesus is very clear about judging: Mat 7:1 'Judge not, that ye be not judged.
:2 For with what judgment ye judge, ye shall be judged: and with what measure ye mete, it shall be measured to you again.'
Luk 6:37 'Judge not, and ye shall not be judged: condemn not, and ye shall not be condemned: forgive, and ye shall be forgiven:'
Paul puts it this way in Romans: Rom 14:10 'But why dost thou judge thy brother? or why dost thou set at nought thy brother? for we shall all stand before the judgment seat of Christ.' In Corinthians he puts it this way: Co 4:5 'Therefore judge nothing before the time, until the Lord come, who both will bring to light the hidden things of

darkness, and will make manifest the counsels of the hearts: and then shall every man have praise of God.' Paul further says: Rom 2:1 'Therefore you are without excuse, O man, everyone who judges; for in that in which you judge another, you condemn yourself, for you who judge do the same things. :2 But know that the judgment of God is according to truth on those who practice such things. :3 And, O man, the one judging those who do such things, and practice them, do you think this, that you shall escape the judgment of God?'

James says: Jas 4:11 'Speak not evil one of another, brethren. He that speaketh evil of his brother, and judgeth his brother, speaketh evil of the law, and judgeth the law: but if thou judge the law, thou art not a doer of the law, but a judge. :12 There is one lawgiver, who is able to save and to destroy: who art thou that judgest another?'

25   Lack of a submissive attitude

Someone once said that the French Revolution might have had many benefits. The feudal system, where there were a few masters and many slaves were over-thrown. The only negative side he said is from then on, everybody wants to be a master and nobody wants to be a servant anymore. Satan demonstrated the same spirit in heaven when he wanted to be like God. He wanted to take His place. Not prepared to serve God anymore. Very often a spirit of rebellion comes up in us when we feel that we must submit to a certain person in authority over us because we feel superior to them. When we feel we can do a much better job than them, why should we listen to them? They should be listening to us.

The Son of the living God, Jesus Christ came to earth to show us what a servant-heart looks like. He could have argued 'why should I, part of the deity, bother with these sinful and stubborn people on earth. Despite this, He chose to come to make us free. He did this to unite us with His heavenly father. He paid the ultimate prize for this by dying on the cross for you and me. Now, God can look at us through the blood of His son (the servant) and not see our sins which were washed away by His blood. All because He was prepared to serve. While on earth, he served by teaching us with sermons, prayers and how to walk our spiritual journey here on earth. The greatest example of practical servanthood was when the saviour of the world washed His disciple's feet. Peter, always knowing better, got caught with his foot in his mouth again, but when he got a better understanding of the matter, he wanted more than what Jesus was going to give:

Joh 13:3 'Jesus knowing that the Father had given all things into his hands, and that he was come from God, and went to God; :4 He riseth from supper, and laid aside his garments; and took a towel, and girded himself. :5 After that he poureth water into a bason, and began to wash the disciples' feet, and to wipe them with the towel wherewith he was girded. :6 Then cometh he to Simon Peter: and Peter saith unto him, Lord, dost thou wash my feet? :7 Jesus answered and said unto him, What I do thou knowest not now; but thou shalt know hereafter. :8 Peter saith unto him, Thou shalt never wash my feet. Jesus answered him, If I wash thee not, thou hast no part with me.

:9 Simon Peter saith unto him, Lord, not my feet only, but also my hands and my head.'
What an example to us humans. When we serve, we want recognition for it. The bible is very clear that we should not seek recognition from men when we serve. Christ says: Mat 6:3 'But when thou doest alms, let not thy left hand know what thy right hand doeth.'
Remember David's attitude towards Saul. David could have killed Saul if he really envied Saul's status and position as king, but David was content with his situation and knew that God would elevate him in His time.

26. Lying

Jesus told the Pharisees that Satan is the father of all lies: Joh 8:44 'Ye are of your father the devil, and the lusts of your father ye will do. He was a murderer from the beginning, and abode not in the truth, because there is no truth in him. When he speaketh a lie, he speaketh of his own: for he is a liar, and the father of it.'
If we lie, we are directly under the control of Satan. That is his territory and he is the master of this domain.
Paul says that if we lie, we are displaying our old nature and not the new nature of Christ in us. Col 3:9 'Lie not one to another, seeing that ye have put off the old man with his deeds; :10 And have put on the new man, which is renewed in knowledge after the image of him that created him:'
God does not like lying: Pro 12:22' Lying lips are abomination to the LORD: but they that deal truly are his delight.'

I think Christians invented the 'white lie'. Women will easily lie about their age. Some men will 'add a little flesh' about their position at work to people who don't know anybody at his work or where he works. Church members might lie about how many members they have in their church. More than often, it is to make us look better or to make the other person feel better. 'Oh, this cake is delicious' while it tastes like a rancid piece of aloe. 'You look so good in that dress' while it looks like she just got out of a laundry basket.

27.   More invested in being heard, than in hearing

How important can our opinions be? How vigorously can we explain to others so that they can understand us? Often not giving the other person a chance to explain their ideas because once they heard and understood our opinion / idea, they will understand that theirs are really inferior.
The author Stephen Covey in his book (Seven habits of highly effective people) suggests that 'we first seek to understand, then to be understood'. We are so scared to give the other person a reasonable opportunity to give his opinion because we just might have to change our long held believes and that would mean that we have lost the argument. To concede would be defeat, and who wants to be a loser?
How often have I run into a brick wall in this area? I would have very strong believes in a certain field till I find myself in conversation with an expert in the field. I would curiously and 'innocently' ask them what their opinion is about a certain matter

(off course not letting them know my long-held firm believes), just to find out that I had 'the cat by the tail'. I would never acknowledge to anyone 'my stinking thinking' on this particular matter, while I have convinced others even less informed than me, to believe my 'rotten ideas' regarding this matter. I can only cry out with the Apostle Paul: Rom 7:24 'O wretched man that I am! who shall deliver me from the body of this death?'

The reason we have TWO ears and ONE mouth might be an indication that we should listen twice as much as we speak.

Pro 10:8 'The wise in heart will receive commandments; but a babbling fool shall fall.'

Pro 20:12 'The hearing ear and the seeing eye, Jehovah has made both of them.'

Jas 1:19 'Therefore, my beloved brothers, let every man be swift to hear, slow to speak, slow to wrath.'

Somebody once said: The biggest communication problem is – We don't listen to Understand, we listen to reply.

28. My way

The times we are living in, is very well described in the Frank Sinatra song 'My way'.
This verse captures it well:
    'I planned each charted course;
    Each careful step along the byway,
    And more, much more than this,
    I did it my way.'

The 'I'. The captain of my own ship. Never seeking God's way.

In Numbers the Israelites are murmuring, they want things to go their way. God says He hears it, and will give them their way. Num 14:27 'How long shall I bear with this evil congregation, which murmur against me? I have heard the murmurings of the children of Israel, which they murmur against me. :28 Say unto them, As truly as I live, saith the LORD, as ye have spoken in mine ears, so will I do to you:'

How often do we do it 'our way' then blame God if the outcome is not favourable? Proverbs describe our way vs God's way like this. Pro 16:2 'All the ways of a man are clean in his own eyes, but Jehovah weighs the spirits.'

Pro 12:15 'The way of a fool is right in his own eyes, but he who listens to advice is wise.'

29.   Babbling

Ecc 10:11 'Surely the serpent will bite without enchantment; and a babbler is no better.' A babbler is not a 'listener'. It is just one flood of 'verbal diarrhea'. I know someone, while babbling himself out of breath, would build is 'pegs' / ideas that he says he will come back to later. In the process basically telling people not to interrupt him, rattling on and on till the others want to fall asleep. A babbler doesn't like to be silenced. According to scripture he is like a serpent that will bite you (get you back somehow) if you dare silence him. Paul advises Timothy against 'idle babbling': 2Ti 2:16 'But shun profane, vain babblings, for they will increase to more ungodliness.'

When the babbler runs out of ideas, they quickly move over to gossip. Ecc 5:2 'Do not be rash with

your mouth, and do not let your heart be hasty to say a word before God. For God is in Heaven, and you are on earth; therefore let your words be few.'
Job 6:24 'Teach me, and I will hold my tongue: and cause me to understand wherein I have erred'.

Job 27:4 'My lips shall not speak wickedness, nor my tongue utter deceit.'

Psa 12:3 'The LORD shall cut off all flattering lips, and the tongue that speaketh proud things:'

Psa 52:2 'Thy tongue deviseth mischiefs; like a sharp razor, working deceitfully.' Psa 119:172 'My tongue shall speak of thy word: for all thy commandments are righteousness.'

If we speak, backed by God's Word, how can we go wrong because it is righteousness? Pro 10:31 'The mouth of the just bringeth forth wisdom: but the froward tongue shall be cut out.' Pro 12:18 'There is that speaketh like the piercings of a sword: but the tongue of the wise is health.'

30.   People pleasing

I remember one day in church when the minister asked the congregation if there were someone who wanted to share something. An elderly lady came forward and told how hard she worked for various charities of the church and that there were people coming against her. At one stage she was crying and said: 'Why can't they see what I'm trying to do for the Lord?'

A family member of mine once told me how she had a grudge against a minister at her church. She worked very hard for an event at her church, when the minister was thanking people

by name that helped with this event, he did not mention her name. I don't think she has forgiven him to this day. All this is people pleasing. We should first please God, and then men will benefit from it.

Mat 6:1 'Take heed that you do not do your merciful deeds before men, to be seen by them. Otherwise you have no reward with your Father in Heaven. :2 Therefore when you do your merciful deeds, do not sound a trumpet before you, as the hypocrites do in the synagogues and in the streets, so that they may have glory from men. Truly I say to you, They have their reward. :3 But when you do merciful deeds, do not let your left hand know what your right hand does, :4 so that your merciful deeds may be in secret. And your Father who sees in secret Himself shall reward you openly.'

In organizations people pleasing can turn ugly as people try to impress the boss. Colleagues can get jealous and start to gossip and spread false rumours against a people-pleaser as to put the person in a bad light with the boss. This could have happened to the elderly lady who started crying in church because her efforts were really focused to please the minister, and he was getting false reports from other helpers and not giving her the praise, she wanted and needed to appease this 'people-pleasing' spirit.

Paul says this is the way we should serve: Col 3:23 'And whatever you do, do it heartily, as to the Lord and not to men; :24 knowing that from the

Lord you shall receive the reward of the inheritance. For you serve the Lord Christ.'

Gal 1:10 'For now do I persuade men, or God? Or do I seek to please men? For if I yet pleased men, I would not be a servant of Christ.'

Eph 6:5 'Slaves, obey your masters according to the flesh, with fear and trembling, in singleness of your heart, as to Christ; :6 not with eye-service, as men-pleasers, but as the servants of Christ, doing the will of God from the heart.'

31.   Perfectionism

Behind perfectionism you will usually find a deep hurt. If I do everything perfect, nobody can criticize me. If I receive criticism, it hurts me deeply. Nobody can reach that wound and pull the scab off. Nobody can catch me off-guard or surprise me. It often ties in with people pleasing. People like this often don't trust anybody to help or do something for them. They do it wrong and not their way. Nobody can do it as well as they do. They're not very flexible personalities. There is only one way and it's their way.

When Jesus visited the two sisters Mary and Martha, they were going to serve Him and His disciples. Mary chose to sit at the feet of Jesus, while Martha ran around like a beheaded chicken trying to do two peoples work. She eventually complained to Jesus about Mary's slackness and not helping her. Martha probably was some sort a perfectionist. She didn't want to be embarrassed about anything. Everything just had to be right to make her feel good.

Luk 10:38 'And as they went, it happened that He entered into a certain village. And a certain woman named Martha received Him into her house. :39 And she had a sister called Mary, who also sat at Jesus' feet and heard His word. :40 But Martha was distracted with much serving. And she came to Him and said, Lord, do You not care that my sister has left me to serve alone? Therefore tell her to help me. :41 And Jesus answered and said to her, Martha, Martha, you are anxious and troubled about many things. :42 But one thing is needful, and Mary has chosen that good part, which shall not be taken away from her.'

In Matthew Jesus calls us to be perfect. Mat 5:48 'Be ye therefore perfect, even as your Father which is in heaven is perfect.'

The English translation lacks the vocabulary, but it isn't the perfect we normally think of. In the Strong Dictionary the definition is: teleios

tel'-i-os

From G5056; complete (in various applications of labor, growth, mental and moral character, etc.); neuter (as noun, with G3588) completeness: - of full age, man, perfect. It is to become complete. To be whole. God will complete His work in us.

Php 1:6 'Being confident of this very thing, that he which hath begun a good work in you will perform it until the day of Jesus Christ.'

32.   Racism

I was born and grew up in South Africa. The government of my day was known worldwide for its policy of Apartheid (Racial Segregation). The white (Caucasian race – of which I'm one) was ruling the country as a minority. Laws applied along racial lines. Signboards at public toilets and restaurants clearly stated 'whites only'. Black and whites weren't treated equally. Blacks had to wear a 'pass' (ID card) all the time and were restricted in their movements. They were not allowed to be in the city streets later than a specific time of night, otherwise they could be arrested. Whites had all the privileges and many believed that they were a superior race to the black people by discriminating against them. Getting rid of such prejudges are not easy. It embeds itself into a whole nation and generation.

Racism has caused many wars and genocide in the world. In Africa tribes have deliberately and systematically tried to wipe each other out, and so in other parts of the world too.

Today South Africa is reaping what it sowed with its apartheid policy. We have a government that consists mainly of a 'struggle generation' that is now practicing discrimination in reverse calling it 'affirmative action'. This very policy has put 'comrades' into positions that they weren't trained or prepared for, with devastating economic and management results. God does not discriminate against races. Gal 3:28 'There is neither Jew nor Greek, there is neither bond nor free, there is neither male nor female: for ye are all one in Christ Jesus.'

We are all one in Christ, regardless of race, colour or gender. God created the first humans (Adam and Eve) in His image. Gen 1:27 'So God created man in his own image, in the image of God created he him; male and female created he them.' From there all humans came. We all have the same roots.

When Christ died on the cross, he did not have a specific race in mind. God offered his Son to all. Joh 3:16 'For God so loved the world, that he gave his only begotten Son, that whosoever believeth in him should not perish, but have everlasting life.'
In the time of Jesus, the Jews could not stand the Samaritans. There was real animosity between them and the Jews looked down on them. They would not be seen having a conversation with them. Jesus was walking through Samaria and stopped at a well to drink water. This is what happened.
Joh 4:5 'Then cometh he to a city of Samaria, which is called Sychar, near to the parcel of ground that Jacob gave to his son Joseph. :6 Now Jacob's well was there. Jesus therefore, being wearied with his journey, sat thus on the well: and it was about the sixth hour. :7 There cometh a woman of Samaria to draw water: Jesus saith unto her, Give me to drink. :8 (For his disciples were gone away unto the city to buy meat.) :9 Then saith the woman of Samaria unto him, How is it that thou, being a Jew, askest drink of me, which am a woman of Samaria? for the Jews have no dealings with the Samaritans. :10 Jesus answered and said unto her, If thou knewest the gift of God, and who it is that saith to thee, Give me to drink; thou wouldest have asked of him, and he would have given thee living water. :11 The woman saith unto him, Sir, thou hast nothing to draw with, and the well is deep: from whence then hast thou that living water? :12 Art thou greater than our father Jacob, which gave us the well, and drank thereof himself, and his children, and his cattle? :13 Jesus

answered and said unto her, Whosoever drinketh of this water shall thirst again: :14 But whosoever drinketh of the water that I shall give him shall never thirst; but the water that I shall give him shall be in him a well of water springing up into everlasting life. :15 The woman saith unto him, Sir, give me this water, that I thirst not, neither come hither to draw. :16 Jesus saith unto her, Go, call thy husband, and come hither. :17 The woman answered and said, I have no husband. Jesus said unto her, Thou hast well said, I have no husband :18 For thou hast had five husbands; and he whom thou now hast is not thy husband: in that saidst thou truly. :19 The woman saith unto him, Sir, I perceive that thou art a prophet. :20 Our fathers worshipped in this mountain; and ye say, that in Jerusalem is the place where men ought to worship. :21 Jesus saith unto her, Woman believe me, the hour cometh, when ye shall neither in this mountain, nor yet at Jerusalem, worship the Father. :22 Ye worship ye know not what: we know what we worship: for salvation is of the Jews. :23 But the hour cometh, and now is, when the true worshippers shall worship the Father in spirit and in truth: for the Father seeketh such to worship him. :24 God is a Spirit: and they that worship him must worship him in spirit and in truth. :25 The woman saith unto him, I know that Messias cometh, which is called Christ: when he is come, he will tell us all things. :26 Jesus saith unto her, I that speak unto thee am he. :27 And upon this came his disciples, and marvelled that he talked with the woman: yet no man said, What seekest thou? or, Why talkest thou with her? :28 The woman then left her waterpot, and went her way into the city, and saith to the men, :29 Come, see a man, which told me all things that ever I did: is not this the Christ? :30 Then they went out of the city, and came unto him. :31 In the mean while his disciples prayed him, saying, Master, eat. :32 But he said unto them, I have meat to eat that ye know not of. :33 Therefore said the disciples one to another, Hath any man brought him ought to eat? :34 Jesus saith unto them, My meat is to do the will of him that sent me, and to finish his work. :35 Say not ye, There are yet four months, and then cometh harvest? behold, I say unto you, Lift up your eyes, and look on the fields; for they are white already to harvest. :36 And he that reapeth receiveth wages, and gathereth fruit unto life eternal: that both he that soweth and he that reapeth may rejoice together. :37 And herein is that saying true, One soweth, and another reapeth. :38 I sent you to reap that whereon ye bestowed no labour: other men laboured, and ye are entered into their labours.:39 And many of the Samaritans of that city believed on him for the saying of the woman, which testified, He told me all that ever I did.'

Even the disciples, who knew Jesus, were surprised that he spoke to this Samaritan woman. Jesus, through His spirit of knowledge new that this woman had many men, and the one she had then, was not her husband, but through her, many in her city believed on Him.

33.   Rebellion

This was Lucifer's downfall. Rebellion. All sin is rebellion against God. All Christians should know what sin is, God builds it into you, and as you study scripture you become more aware of what is wrong without being 'sin conscious' all the time. Once you are a blood washed and baptized child of God, you are free, yes even free to sin sometimes, but the Holy Spirit will convict you. You then ask forgiveness and move on without quilt. You are forgiven! The load has been shed, and you walk lightly and purposefully. Don't let anybody remind you of that sin again – Satan will, but you can quote scripture like Romans 8: 1-2: 'There is therefore now no condemnation to them which are in Christ Jesus, who walk not after the flesh, but after the Spirit. For the law of the Spirit of life in Christ Jesus hath made me free from the law of sin and death.'

As we know, Satan rebelled against God and was cast out of heaven with a third of the angels. How often do we rebel against authority (parent, school, workplace, church and government)?

David's son, Absalom rebelled against his father. He wanted to take over the kingship of David by organizing a revolt against his father. He was so successful that David had to flee from his son. In 2 Samuel we read about this rebel-rouser and his plotting and scheming. Absalom had beautiful long hair, while he was riding his mule through trees, the following happened:

2 Sa 18:9 'And Absalom met the servants of David. And Absalom rode upon a mule, and the mule went under the thick boughs of a great oak, and his head caught hold of the oak, and he was taken up between the heaven and the earth; and the mule that was under him went away.'

There he hung till he died. That was his reward for rebellion against his father.

Churches also split up because of this spirit of rebellion, usually led by an Absalom who want things his way. Like Absalom and Satan, they gather support by lies and half-truths to make sure they don't end up standing alone but have support (there is safety in numbers), and then start their own church or movement. This goes on and on in churches hence the thousands of denominations and movements. The devil's policy is: divide and rule.

Ezekiel 28 talks about the prince of Tyrus, which some scholars reckon could be Satan. We read how his heart was lifted up (arrogance, pride). Eze 28:13 'Thou hast been in Eden the garden of God; every precious stone was thy covering, the sardius, topaz, and the diamond, the beryl, the onyx, and the jasper, the sapphire, the emerald, and the carbuncle, and gold: the workmanship of thy tabrets and of thy pipes was prepared in thee in the day that thou wast created.:14 Thou art the anointed cherub that covereth; and I have set thee so: thou wast upon the holy mountain of God; thou hast walked up and down in the midst of the stones of fire. :15 Thou wast perfect in thy ways from the day that thou wast created, till iniquity was found in thee. :16 By the multitude of thy merchandise they have filled the midst of thee with violence, and thou hast sinned: therefore I will cast thee as profane out of the mountain of God: and I will destroy thee, O covering cherub, from the midst of the stones of fire.:17 Thine heart was lifted up because of thy beauty, thou hast corrupted thy wisdom by reason of thy brightness: I will cast thee to the ground, I will lay thee before kings, that they may behold thee. :18 Thou hast defiled thy sanctuaries by the multitude of thine iniquities, by the iniquity of thy traffick; therefore will I bring forth a fire from the midst of thee, it shall devour thee, and I will bring thee to ashes upon the earth in the sight of all them that behold thee.'

The Psalmist says this about the rebellious: Psa 68:6 'God setteth the solitary in families: he bringeth out those which are bound with chains: but the rebellious dwell in a dry land.'
In Proverbs: Pro 17:11 'An evil man seeketh only rebellion: therefore a cruel messenger shall be sent against him.'

Paul writes to Timothy how we should treat those in authority. We have to pray for them.
1Ti 2:1 'I exhort therefore, that, first of all, supplications, prayers, intercessions, and giving of thanks, be made for all men; :2 For kings, and for all that are in authority; that we may lead a quiet and peaceable life in all godliness and honesty. :3 For this is good and acceptable in the sight of God our Saviour; :4 Who will have all men to be saved, and to come unto the knowledge of the truth.'
We must earnestly pray for those in authority for Godly wisdom, knowledge, insight and revelation. Those that don't know the saviour shall meet Him and then govern in a righteous manner.

I do believe though, that we as individuals should resist sinning, if that is what authorities require of us. The questions how do we as Christians react to laws like abortion and same-sex marriage which is clearly a violation of God's word? I really don't know if marches and protests will change anything. The argument would simply be 'it is legalized and you stick to the rules or face the court and jail'. Maybe the solution is prayer, to speak and preach, and motivate why we are against it. To live as an example, and invoke others to jealousy.

34. Revenge

In the time of Ahab and Jezebel, the prophet Elijah prayed for drought because of the King and his wife's wickedness. Elijah spoke to Ahab to organize a public event to test who the true God is. Is it Baal, or the God of Israel? Elijah challenged 450 Baal priests to meet him on Mount Carmel to proof who the living God is.
We read about this event in 1 Kings 18. The Baal priests built and altar and had a bull on it, so did Elijah. None of the two parties were to light the fire for the offering, but to pray to their God to do it for them. Here is the account of what happened there.
1Ki 18:20 'And Ahab sent to all the sons of Israel, and gathered the prophets together to mount Carmel. :21 And Elijah came to all the people and said, How long are you limping over two opinions? If Jehovah is God, follow Him. But if Baal is God, then follow him. And the people did not answer him a word. :22 And Elijah said to the people, I, I alone, remain a prophet of Jehovah. But Baal's prophets are four hundred and fifty men. ;23 And let them give us two bulls, and let them choose one bull for themselves, and cut it in pieces and lay it on wood. But place no fire. And I will dress the other bull and lay it on wood, and place no fire. :24 And you call on the name of your gods, and I will call on the name of Jehovah. And it shall be, the god that answers by fire, He is

God. And all the people answered and said, The word is good. :25 And Elijah said to the prophets of Baal, Choose one bull for yourselves, and prepare first, for you are many. And call on the name of your god, but place no fire. :26 And they took the bull which was given them, and they dressed, and called on the name of Baal from morning even until noon, saying, O Baal, hear us. But there was no voice, nor any who answered. And they leaped on the altar which was made. :27 And it happened at noon Elijah mocked them and said, Cry with a great voice, for he is a god. Either he is meditating, or he is pursuing, or he is in a journey; perhaps he is asleep and must be awakened! :28 And they cried with a loud voice and cut themselves with knives and spears until the blood gushed out on them, as is their way. :29 And it happened when midday was past, and when they prophesied until the time of the offering of the evening sacrifice, there was neither voice, nor any to answer, nor anyone who paid attention. :30 And Elijah said to all the people, Come near to me. And all the people came near him. And he repaired the broken down altar of Jehovah. :31 And Elijah took twelve stones, according to the number of the tribes of the sons of Jacob, to whom the Word of Jehovah came, saying, Israel shall be your name. :32 And with stones he built an altar in the name of Jehovah. And he made a trench around the altar big enough to contain two measures of seed. :33 And he arranged the wood, and cut the bull in pieces, and placed it on the wood, and said, Fill four water jars with water and pour on the burnt sacrifice and on the wood. :34 And he said, Do it the second time. And they did it the second time.

And he said, Do it the third time. And they did it the third time. :35 And the water ran all around the altar. And he filled the trench also with water. :36 And it happened at the time of the offering of the evening sacrifice, Elijah the prophet came near and said, Jehovah, the God of Abraham, Isaac, and of Israel, let it be known this day that You are God in Israel, and that I am Your servant, and that I have done all these things at Your Word. :37 Hear me, O Jehovah, hear me, that this people may know that You are Jehovah God, and that You have turned their heart back again. :38 And the fire of Jehovah fell and burned up the burnt sacrifice and the wood, and the stones and the dust, and licked up the water that was in the trench. :39 And when all the people saw, they fell on their faces. And they said, Jehovah, He is the God! Jehovah, He is the God! :40 And Elijah said to them, Take the prophets of Baal. Do not let one of them escape. And they took them. And Elijah brought them down to the torrent Kishon and killed them there. :41 And Elijah said to Ahab, Go up, eat and drink, because of the sound of plenty of rain :42 So Ahab went up to eat and to drink. And Elijah went up to the top of Carmel. And he threw himself down on the earth and put his face between his knees. :43 And he said to his servant, Go up now, look toward the sea. And he went up and looked and said, Nothing. And he said, Go again seven times. :44 And it happened at the seventh time, he said, Behold, there arises a little cloud out of the sea, like a man's hand. And he said, Go up and say to Ahab, Bind up and go down, so that the rain does not stop you. :45 And it happened in the meantime the heaven was black with clouds and wind, and there was a great rain. And Ahab rose and went to Jezreel. :46 And the hand of Jehovah was on Elijah. And he girded up his loins and ran before Ahab to the entrance of Jezreel.'

The God of Israel and Elijah made a public spectacle of the false god Baal and his prophets. God revealed Himself as the true and only God. Elijah, knowing that Jezebel is going to take revenge on him, ran for his life. This after he clearly saw what his God can do. The fear of Jezebel was just overwhelming to this great prophet of God. That is what the fear of revenge can do to us sometimes. Not believing that God can protect us. Here is the account what happened after Elijah killed the Baal false prophets. 1Ki 19:1 'And Ahab told Jezebel all that Elijah had done, and withal how he had slain all the prophets with the sword. :2 Then Jezebel sent a messenger unto Elijah, saying, So let the gods do to me, and more also, if I make not thy life as the life of one of them by tomorrow about this time. :3 And when he saw that, he arose, and went for his life, and came to Beersheba, which belongeth to Judah, and left his servant there. :4 But he himself went a day's journey into the wilderness, and came and sat down under a juniper tree: and he requested for himself that he might die; and said, It is enough; now, O LORD, take away my life; for I am not better than my fathers.'

When my son was about 15 years old (I was divorced from his mother when he was 9), his mother went to a conference about 1500km away. He stayed alone in the apartment for about 2 days. It was a fenced-in development. Where their apartment was, there wasn't a wall but a barbed wire fence between them and a vineyard. One night while he was sleeping, thugs came through the fence, got entry through a window and held him up with a gun while they cleaned the apartment of valuables, put it in her car, tied him up, and left. The police found the car abandoned in a township about 40 km from there. His wrists were cut as he tried to wrestle himself loose and kicked the door in where they locked him in. He then phoned the police.

I had a job then where I drove around all day and had a lot of time to think. I was so enraged about the situation and the lawlessness and crime in South Africa that I devised all kinds of plans to take revenge. At one stage I even thought of a plan to capture the Minister of Security and do the same to him so he can experience firsthand the criminality gripping the country. My heart was full of hate and vengeance. I thought what I would do to the criminals who did this. On and on' day and night, I was plotting and scheming, with hate ever increasing.

About three weeks later I was sitting in church and the minister was talking about forgiveness. I realized that I was a victim in this case. My heart and mind were bound by hate and vengeance. The criminals didn't even know me and what I felt and planned. I was in my own prison and they were walking free probably bragging to their fellow thug friends what a nice robbery they pulled off while I was busy polluting my mind, heart body and soul with revenge and hate. I immediately asked God forgiveness - forgave the criminals and asked God to intervene in their lives, and I was set free to busy my mind with better thoughts.

35. Self-centeredness, Self-obsession and Self-pity

The self, the I, the me and myself. Together we can have a nice pity party. We can withdraw into our little shell, hard as the skin of Leviathan (Job 41). We don't want anybody in, it is our own little 'private space' where we can meditate and ponder about all the wrongs that has been perpetrated against us. Where we can mill and maul about issues, chew and re-chew thoughts about how unfair people and life can be against us. And of-course the enemy (Satan) keeps on adding new issues to the existing ones. So, we go down in a maelstrom and the focus is Self. Our perspective is blinded by ourselves and our adversary, the devil. Inside ourselves we hear: I don't need advice from anybody now – I don't want to hear any 'bible punchers' counseling me, I will sort this out by myself. All we want to do is to dump our bitterness and often unforgiveness on somebody without hearing any advice or counseling in return. I know exactly what the reason is for my sadness, it is because so and so did / said this to / about me. It is because God is favouring so and so above me. We spin ourselves into a cocoon and the Leviathan spirit comes and seals it with his scales. Job 41:15   'His scales are his pride, shut up together as with a close seal.'

Self-pity is self-centeredness, an obsession with ourselves, and the root is pride. Satan wants your attention focused on yourself and the injustices done to you. It robs God of your praises and thanksgiving. Because, really you know, how can I be praising anything in these circumstances? Once I get over it and get 'back to normal' I will start worshipping and spending time with God. I just want to 'ride this wave out', and then everything will be back to 'normal' again.

Ahab displayed this very behaviour when Naboth wouldn't sell him his vineyard. He also didn't eat to draw attention to himself. So, people (especially his wife) can take pity. So, she and others can sympathize with him. To point out the grave injustice done to him. 1Ki 21:4 'And Ahab came into his house heavy and displeased because of the word which Naboth the Jezreelite had spoken to him: for he had said, I will not give thee the inheritance of my fathers. And he laid him down upon his bed, and turned away his face, and would eat no bread. :5 But Jezebel his wife came to him, and said unto him, Why is thy spirit so sad, that thou eatest no bread?'

Even the great patron of patience and endurance, Job, fell into self-pity. We often hear people would refer to someone saying: he/she has the patience of a Job.

Here is what God said about Job. Job 1:8 'And Jehovah said to Satan, Have you set your heart against My servant Job, because there is none like him in the earth, a perfect and upright man, one who fears God and turns away from evil? :9 And Satan answered Jehovah and said, Does Job fear God for nothing? :10 Have You not made a hedge around him, and around his house, and around all that he has on every side? You have blessed the work of his hands, and his livestock have increased in the land.'

'None like him – perfect and upright man'. God 'made a hedge around him'.

Job was a prosperous man, then came a day of calamity: Job 1:13 'And a day came when his sons and his daughters were eating and drinking wine in their oldest brother's house. :14 And there came a messenger to Job and said, The oxen were plowing, and the asses feeding beside them. :15 And the Sabeans fell on and took them away. Yea, they have killed the servants with the edge of the sword. And I only have escaped alone to tell you. :16 While he was still speaking, there also came another and said, The fire of God has fallen from the heavens and has burned up the sheep and the servants, and destroyed them. And I only have escaped alone to tell you. :17 While he was still speaking, there also came another and said, The Chaldeans made out three bands and swooped down upon the camels, and have carried them away, yea, and have killed the servants with the edge of the sword. And I only have escaped alone to tell you. :18 While he was still speaking, there also came another and said, Your sons and your daughters were eating and drinking wine in their oldest brother's house. :19 And, behold, a great wind came from the wilderness and struck the four corners of the house, and it fell upon the young men, and they are dead. And I only have escaped alone to tell you.'

Job first reaction was not anger or the 'blaming game'. No, he ran to the source he knew that would comfort him: Job 1:20 'And Job arose, and tore his robe, and shaved his head, and fell down upon the ground and worshiped. :21 And he said, I came naked out of my mother's womb, and naked shall I return there. Jehovah gave, and Jehovah has taken away. Blessed be the name of Jehovah. Later on though, we do find Job complaining and falling into self-pity. Job 3:1 'After this Job opened his mouth and cursed his day. :2 And Job spoke and said, :3 Let the day perish in which I was born, and the night which said, A man-child is conceived. :4 Let that day be darkness. Let not God look upon it from above, neither let the light shine upon it. :5 Let darkness and the shadow of death claim it. Let a cloud dwell upon it; Let the blackness of the day terrify it. :6 As for that night, let darkness seize upon it. Let it not rejoice among the days of the year, Let it not come into the number of the months. :7 Lo, let that night be barren; let no joyful voice come in it. :8 Let those curse it who curse the day, who are ready to stir up Leviathan. :9 Let the stars of its twilight be dark; let it look for light, but have none. Let it not see the eyelids of the dawn. :10 For it did not shut up the doors of my mother's womb, nor hide sorrow from my eyes :11 Why did I not die from the womb, come from the womb and expire?'

Job 7:13 'When I say, My bed shall comfort me, my couch shall ease my complaint, :14 then You scare me with dreams, and terrify me with visions; :15 so that my soul chooses strangling, death rather than my life. :16 I despise them; I will not live always; let me alone, for my days are vanity.'

Job 19:21 'Have pity on me! Have pity on me, my friends! For the hand of God has touched me.'

I remember when I was going through great financial difficulty and I could see that this thing isn't going to end well. I was in a great wrestling-match with God like Jacob in the bible was in his dream. Sunday's I use to have a nap and after that I would go for a long walk to try and clear my mind and talk to God. It is a very beautiful part of South

Africa and I would walk up the mountain from where one has a beautiful view of the sea and the mountains. I was really in the grip of fear and self-pity. I had property in another town with a tenant in it. It was part of my investment plan for retirement one day. I had a cash investment in a fund that grew well. I first sold the property so I could live of the profit I made. That money was now eaten up, and I realized I will have to start drawing from my investment. I got the feeling that the writing was on the wall. This particular Sunday was heavy for me. I asked God to give me just a ray of hope because I am sinking very fast into financial and emotional ruin. I was on my way back home and came around a corner of a house with a high brick wall. As I came around the corner there was a little boy about 4 years old holding onto a wrought iron gate like a prisoner peeping through prison-bars. He only said two words: 'Hello uncle'. It hit me like a tidal wave. I don't know why. There was something coming out of that child's voice which I cannot describe in words. I kindly greeted him back and walked on. I felt as light as a feather. I believe that God spoke to me through that child. That kid probably will never know what he meant to me, and that God used him. Bless him.

Mat 11:25 'At that time Jesus answered and said, I thank You, O Father, Lord of Heaven and earth, because You have hidden these things from the sophisticated and cunning, and revealed them to babes.' Mat 21:16 'And they said to Him, Do you hear what these say? And Jesus said to them, Yes, have you never read, "Out of the mouth of babes and sucklings You have perfected praise?'

When we give our lives to Jesus, we get a new life. The 'old man' is dead. Paul puts it this way: Rom 6:3 'Know ye not, that so many of us as were baptized into Jesus Christ were baptized into his death? :4 Therefore we are buried with him by baptism into death: that like as Christ was raised up from the dead by the glory of the Father, even so we also should walk in newness of life. :5 For if we have been planted together in the likeness of his death, we shall be also in the likeness of his resurrection: 6 Knowing this, that our old man is crucified with him, that the body of sin might be destroyed, that henceforth we should not serve sin. :7 For he that is dead is freed from sin.'

Rom 8:5 'For they that are after the flesh do mind the things of the flesh; but they that are after the Spirit the things of the Spirit. :6 For to be carnally minded is death; but to be spiritually minded is life and peace. :7 Because the carnal mind is enmity against God: for it is not subject to the law of God, neither indeed can be. :8 So then they that are in the flesh cannot please God.'

Isn't Paul trying to tell us here, that something like self-pity means walking in the flesh (carnally minded) and not in the spirit? Further Paul says that we should renew our minds: Rom 12:2 'And be not conformed to this world: but be ye transformed by the renewing of your mind, that ye may prove what is that good, and acceptable, and perfect, will of God.'

How often we start pitying ourselves when someone points us to sin in our lives; who are you to correct me?; often followed by revenge and shunning that person, sometimes gossiping about them and pointing to flaws in their lives to counter and disguise our own sins. We can cast this sorrowful spirit out and send it to dry places where Jesus will deal with it: 1Sa 1:15 'And Hannah answered, No, my lord, I am a woman of a sorrowful spirit. I have neither drunk wine nor strong drink, but have poured out my soul before Jehovah.'

Look where Hannah took her problem. She recognized this spirit and took it before the Lord. He turned the sorrowful spirit into a joyful one in such a way that she appeared drunk.

Think about the 'selfie' phenomena these days. Surely nothing wrong with taking a picture of yourself now and again, but it seems like some people are totally obsessed by it.

36. <u>Shyness</u>

Hard to believe, but more often than not, shyness can be a form of pride. That shield of Leviathan we build around us. No-one can get in. We don't want to show our true colours, because people can correct and reprimand us. We might say something wrong that can get us into troubled water and we might have to apologize, or it might be proof that we are not very clever or informed about a matter. We shouldn't confuse shyness with modesty. Modesty is where people don't go around boasting about their achievements and successes. Shyness usually manifests itself where the person deliberately doesn't act or say something because they fear the consequences.

We know by now who sits behind fear, yes, the enemy (Satan) himself. We have seen how many kinds of fears and phobias there are. From the fear of love to the fear of rejection, the fear of money and the fear of a lack thereof, the fear to live and to the fear to die. The opposite of fear is faith and trust. 1Jn 4:18 'There is no fear in love, but perfect love casts out fear, because fear has torment. He who fears has not been perfected in love.'

Paul puts it this way: 2Ti 1:7 'For God has not given us the spirit of fear, but of power and of love and of a sound mind.'

The book of Hebrews talks about how important faith is: Heb 11:6 'But without faith it is impossible to please Him, for he who comes to God must believe that He is and that He is a rewarder of those who diligently seek Him.'

Shy people often creep out of their Leviathan scaled skin when they had taken some intoxicating substance like alcohol. Then the shyness is gone, and they can be very talkative and 'witty'. That is why the scripture says: Eph 5:18 'And be not drunk with wine, wherein is excess; but be filled with the Spirit.'

The Holy Spirit is a cure for shyness. We saw in 1Sa 1:15 that Hannah appeared drunk when she was in front of Jehovah and poured her soul out.

Shyness can rob us of friendships and healthy relationships. It can prevent us from getting divine appointments in business. It can make good people avoid us because they know we retreat into our cave and no useful interaction can take place. Shyness will limit our spiritual growth. It will prevent us from sharing troubling matters with fellow Christians and earnestly look for solutions. It will prevent us from being of any service to our brethren because we avoid situations where God can use us powerfully in ministering to others in church and bible study groups.

Paul says: Rom 1:16 'For I am not ashamed of the gospel of Christ, for it is the power of God unto salvation to everyone who believes, to the Jew first and also to the Greek.'

37. Stealing

We think of stealing generally as taking something that does not belong to us without the owner's consent, and making it our own. Yes, that is stealing, but there are many other ways of stealing. Stealing someone's idea/s, pretending it was our own brilliant discovery, sometimes things like a patent and making lots of money from it. Other times just pretending it was something we figured out because we're so clever, meantime stealing from someone else. One of the Ten Commandments states clearly that we are not to steal. Short and simple.

Exo 20:15 'You shall not steal.' I know people who would hear something for the first time from someone, then would tell it at another event as if it happened to them. Not only lying, but stealing a story and ideas from others, trying to make them important and being the center of attention. When we have an affair outside of wedlock we are stealing. If a man has a relationship with another man's wife, he is stealing the other man' glory. A wife is a husband's glory. Also, if a married woman

has an affair with another man, she takes (steals) her husband's glory and give's it to another man. How often do we 'steal' our employers time by playing games on the computer, chatting on Facebook, sending emails to friends and family? Eph 4:28 'Let him who stole steal no more, but rather let him labor, working with his hands the thing which is good, so that he may have something to give to him who needs.'
Paul is suggesting that we work for what we have, and more than that, so we can have overflow and share and give to those in need. Yes, many people steal because they are too lazy to work and wait for others to provide for them.
Worst of all, we often try to steal God's glory. Satan, as we have seen, has tried to lift himself to the status, and maybe, even higher, than God. It did not work out well for him. For King Nebuchadnezzar things also didn't turn out so well when he marvelled in his own abilities and not giving credit to God. Dan 4:30 'The king spoke and said, Is this not great Babylon that I have built for the house of the kingdom by the might of my power and for the honor of my majesty? :31 While the word was in the king's mouth, a voice fell from Heaven, saying, O King Nebuchadnezzar, to you it is spoken. The kingdom has departed from you. :32 And they shall drive you from men, and your dwelling shall be with the animals of the field. They shall make you eat grass like oxen, and seven times shall pass over you, until you know that the Most High rules in the kingdom of men, and gives it to whomever He will: 33 The same hour the thing was fulfilled on Nebuchadnezzar. And he was driven from men, and ate grass like oxen, and his body was wet with the dew of the heavens,

until his hair had grown like eagles' feathers, and his nails like birds' claws.'

In the end, Nebuchadnezzar realized his mistake that he did not give God the glory He deserved, and wanted all the recognition and praise for himself and repented, and God restored him. Dan 4:34 'And at the end of days, I Nebuchadnezzar lifted up my eyes to Heaven, and my understanding returned to me, and I blessed the Most High, and I praised and honored Him who lives forever, whose kingdom is an everlasting kingdom, and His rule is from generation to generation. :35 And all the people of the earth are counted as nothing; and He does according to His will in the army of heaven, and among the people of the earth. And none can strike His hand, or say to Him, What are You doing? :36 At that time my reason returned to me. And the glory of my kingdom, my honor and brightness returned to me. And my advisers and my lords came for me, and I was established in my kingdom, and excellent majesty was added to me. :37 Now I Nebuchadnezzar praise and exalt and honor the King of heaven, all whose works are truth and His ways judgment. And those who walk in pride He is able to humble.'

Many ministries today bare the name of a person like: Joe Soap Ministries. Really? Does Joe tell them about himself, or does he proclaim the gospel of Jesus Christ? Is the focus on Jesus, or on Joe Soap? Does he claim the converts and the healed for Joe, or for the kingdom of Jesus Christ? Most of the offerings and donations go to enrich Joe and his family rather than benefit the family of Christ. The money goes for more TV time, jets to fly him and his ever-growing support staff quickly around to some big payday-event at a bigger and bigger stadium which means more income to spend on a bigger or a second holiday- home somewhere pristine, and of course the necessary cars to fit his status. A quick prayer and a blessing from Joe (after you gave a handsome offering of course) can put you in the pound seats very soon. Yes, it's going well with Joe financially. Let's not worry too much about the bewildered and confused who come to meet the Living Christ at his meetings. Make your offering, and if you're confused, just keep on seeking, is the basic message. All for the glory of self. Using and abusing God for a quick buck and self-enrichment, stealing God's glory for personal interests. Leaving people thinking God is an ATM where you can make a quick withdrawal without investing anything. God does not share His glory with no-one.

We are called to give glory to God and Him only. That is why He created us. Anything else is Idolatry. God is speaking through Isaiah: Isa 48:11 'For my sake, for My sake I will do it; for why should My name be defiled? And I will not give My glory to another.'

When God talks about: 'for My or My name's sake, He is talking about His glory.

Psa 79:9 'Help us, O God of our salvation, for the glory of Your name; and deliver us, and atone for our sins, for Your name's sake.'

Psa 106:8 'But He saved them for His name's sake, to make His mighty power known.'

Psa 115:1 'Not to us, O Jehovah, not to us, but to Your name give glory, for Your mercy and for Your truth's sake.'

Isa 43:25 'I, I am He who blots out your sins for My own sake, and will not remember your sins.'
Dan 9:15 'And now, O Lord our God, who have brought Your people out from the land of Egypt with a mighty hand, and have brought fame to Yourself, as it is today, we have sinned, we have done wrong.'
Eze 38:23 'So I will magnify Myself and sanctify Myself. And I will be known in the eyes of many nations, and they shall know that I am Jehovah.'
Isa 55:8 'For My thoughts are not your thoughts, nor your ways My ways, says Jehovah.'
Isa 55:9 'For as the heavens are higher than the earth, so are My ways higher than your ways, and My thoughts than your thoughts'.
2Co 4:7 'But we have this treasure in earthen vessels, so that the excellence of the power may be of God and not of us.'
Paul says: 2Co 12:10 'Therefore I am pleased in weaknesses, in insults, in necessities, in persecutions, in distresses for Christ's sake; for when I am weak, then I am powerful.'
Joh 15:4 'Abide in Me, and I in you. As the branch cannot bear fruit of itself unless it remains in the vine, so neither can you unless you abide in Me.'
So, beloved of God, do NOT steal God's glory. There is neither fruit nor salvation there.

38.   Stinginess vs Giving

Stinginess is a matter of the heart, often driven by fear. If I give to you, you might have more than me and that is no good. If I give to you, I might have lack and must go without. If I give to you, it might become a habit and you will keep on coming back again and again. Endless arguments and excuses not to give. What we are really saying is: God, I don't believe you can provide for me. If I give, there is no source where I can eat and drink from.

Gen 13:1 'And Abram went up out of Egypt, he, and his wife, and all that he had, (and Lot was with him) into the south. :2 And Abram was very rich in cattle, in silver and in gold. :3 And he went on his journeys from the south, even to Bethel, to the place where his tent had been from the beginning, between Bethel and Hai, :4 to the place of the altar which he had made there at the first. And Abram called on the name of Jehovah there. :5 And Lot, who went with Abram, also had flocks and herds and tents. :6 And the land was not able to bear them, that they might live together. For their substance was great, so that they could not live together. :7 And there was strife between the herdsmen of Abram's cattle and the herdsmen of Lot's cattle. And the Canaanite and the Perizzite lived then in the land. :8 And Abram said to Lot, Let there be no strife, I pray you, between me and you, and between my herdsmen and your herdsmen; for we are men, brothers. :9 Is not the whole land before you? I pray you, separate yourself from me. If you go to the left, then I will go to the right. Or if you go to the right, then I will go to the left. :10 And Lot lifted up his eyes and saw all the circuit of Jordan, that it was all well watered (before Jehovah destroyed Sodom and Gomorrah,) like the garden of Jehovah, like the land of Egypt as you come to Zoar. :11 And Lot chose all the circuit of Jordan for himself. And Lot journeyed east; and they separated themselves from one another.'

Here we have the story of Abram and his nephew Lot. Abram could have chosen the best land for himself, but out of generosity and his faith that God will bless him under any circumstance, he let Lot choose first, and so Lot chose the best.

Consider this: God asked Abraham to offer his long awaited and only son, Isaac. This must have been a terrible blow to him, but he obeyed and God gave the ram to be offered just before Abraham could light the fire with Isaac bound on top of it.
Gen 22:1 'And it happened after these things that God tested Abraham, and said to him, Abraham! And he said, Behold me. :2 And He said, Take now your son, your only one, Isaac, whom you love. And go into the land of Moriah, and offer him there for a burnt offering upon one of the mountains which I will name to you.'

This was a shadow of what was to come. God offered His only Son on Mount Calgary, apparently not far from where Abraham was going to offer Isaac. What God is trying to tell us, is to see and feel the agony that Abraham had to go through sacrificing his only son, but God spared Isaac, but not His only Son Jesus. That is the price that God paid and gave to mankind. Unfortunately, not all accept this offer, which I think grieves God as much as when He gave His son to be crucified. Through this act of giving from God the Father, and Jesus accepting that He will be the lamb to be offered, we are now united with the living God through the cross and the blood of Jesus. Washed clean and holy before God. Joh 3:16 'For God so loved the world that He gave His only-begotten

Son, that whoever believes in Him should not perish but have everlasting life. 1 Jn 3:16 'By this we have known the love of God, because He laid down His life for us. And we ought to lay down our lives for the brothers.'

There are so many scriptures which encourages us to give. To be charitable and caring and help where we can. It does not necessarily mean we have to give money, but we can give things we have like food, clothes and of course, our time in counseling, listening and praying with those in need.

Luk 6:38 'Give, and it shall be given to you, good measure pressed down and shaken together and running over, they shall give into your bosom. For with the same measure that you measure, it shall be measured to you again.'
In the book of Acts, Luke tells us not to be lazy. Do not sit around doing nothing and expect others to give to you, and if they don't, you accuse them of being stingy. Act 20:33 'I have coveted no man's silver or gold or apparel. :34 Yea, you yourselves know that these hands have ministered to my needs, and to those who were with me. :35 I have shown you all things, that working in this way we ought to help the weak, and to remember the words of the Lord Jesus, that He Himself said, It is more blessed to give than to receive.'
Heb 13:2 'Do not be forgetful of hospitality, for by this some have entertained angels without knowing it.'
How many times have I missed out on this opportunity? Forgive me God. I have often told people, I can't be in the hospitality business

because it irritates me when you come across people who nag, moan and groan all the time. You can never please them. I live in Asia now while writing this book. I have lived in Asia for more than six years. Their hospitality is remarkable. They would always insist that you drink tea, or have a meal with them. It always reminds me of the early church where they had the 'common meal' together. Never letting anybody leave hungry or thirsty.

Tit 2:14 'who gave Himself for us that He might redeem us from all iniquity and purify to Himself a special people, zealous of good works.'

Pro 11:25 'The soul who gives freely shall be made fat; and he who waters shall also be watered himself.'

2Co 8:9 'For you know the grace of our Lord Jesus Christ, that, though He was rich, for your sakes He became poor, in order that you might be made rich through His poverty.'

Joh 16:24 'Before now you have asked nothing in My name; ask and you shall receive, that your joy may be full.'

This verse is important to those who are always waiting to receive. Ask that the Lord will bless you so you can be a giver.

Paul says if you sow generously, so will your harvest be. Be generous to those who labour in the field for the Lord, like missionaries, going to places where few people are prepared to go and proclaim the 'Good news'. There is a blessing in store for you.

2Co 9:6 'But I say this, He who sows sparingly shall also reap sparingly, and he who sows bountifully shall also reap bountifully. :7 Each one, as he purposes in his heart, let him give; not of grief, or of necessity, for God loves a cheerful giver. :8 And God is able to make all grace abound toward you, that in everything, always having all self-sufficiency, you may abound to every good work; :9 As it is written, "He scattered; he has given to the poor; his righteousness remains forever." :10 Now He who supplies seed to the sower, and bread for eating, may He supply and multiply your seed, and increase the fruits of your righteousness :11 you being enriched in everything to all generosity, which works out thanksgiving to God through us. :12 For the ministry of this service not only supplies the things lacking of the saints, but also multiplying through many thanksgivings to God, :13 through the proof of this ministry they glorify God for your freely expressed submission to the gospel of Christ, and the generosity of the fellowship toward them and toward all, :14 and in their prayer for you, who long after you, because of the exceeding grace of God on you. :15 Thanks be to God for His unspeakable free gift.'

39. Stubbornness

Deu 21:18 'If a man has a son who is stubborn and rebels, who will not obey his father's voice or his mother's voice, even when they have chastened him he will not listen to them, :19 then his father and his mother shall lay hold on him and bring him out to the elders of his city, and to the gate of his place. :20 And they shall say to the elders of his city, this son of ours is stubborn and rebellious. He will not obey our voice. He is a glutton and a drunkard. :21 And all the men of his city shall stone him with stones so that he dies. So shall you put evil away from you, and all Israel shall hear and fear.'

Quite a hard punishment for stubbornness, and clearly a sign that it is not a good thing to do. Stubbornness and rebellion usually are close friends. They work hand in hand. This is what Samuel told Saul because of his rebellion, stubbornness and disobedience: 1Sa 15:23 'For rebellion is as the sin of witchcraft, and stubbornness is as iniquity and idol-worship. Because you have rejected the Word of Jehovah, He has also rejected you from being king!' Rebellion is like witchcraft. That is a scary thought. Christians do witchcraft with witches and the devil himself, without realizing that it is on an equal footing as rebellion.
2Ki 17:13 'And Jehovah testified against Israel, and against Judah, by all the prophets, by all the seers, saying, Turn from your evil ways and keep My commandments, My statutes, according to all the Law which I commanded your fathers, and which I sent to you by My servants the prophets. :14 But they would not hear, but hardened their necks, like the neck of their fathers who did not believe in Jehovah their God.'
They 'hardened their necks' (rebellion) against the Lord by not walking in His ways. They went after other gods. That is what rebellion does. We refuse to follow God and fall into idolatry. When we walk out of line with God's statues and laws, we fall into witchcraft trying to manipulate and control our way forward.

Paul puts it this way: Eph 4:17 'This I say therefore, and testify in the Lord, that you should not walk from now on as other nations walk, in the vanity of their mind, :18 having the understanding darkened, being alienated from the life of God through the ignorance that is in them, because of the blindness of their heart.'

Nehemiah put it this way: Neh 9:16 'But they and our fathers acted proudly and hardened their necks, and did not listen to Your commandments. :17 And they refused to obey, neither were they mindful of Your wonders which You did among them. But they hardened their necks, and in their rebellion appointed a captain to return to their bondage. But You are a God ready to pardon, gracious and merciful, slow to anger, and of great kindness, and did not forsake them.'

If we are stiff-necked / rebellious, we resist the Holy Spirit: Act 7:51 'O stiff-necked and uncircumcised in heart and ears! You always resist the Holy Spirit. As your fathers did, so you do.'

Stubbornness is the opposite of righteousness. Isa 46:12 'Listen to me, stubborn-hearted who are far from righteousness.'
Here is the result of stubbornness: Psa 81:11 'But My people would not listen to My voice, and Israel would have none of Me. :12 So I gave them up to the stubbornness of their own hearts; and they walked in their own conceits.'
The perfect example of someone who wasn't stubborn and didn't rebel against God, was Jesus: Joh 5:30 'I can do nothing of My own self. As I hear, I judge, and My judgment is just, because I

do not seek My own will, but the will of the Father who has sent Me.'
The pride of stubbornness will prevent us of confessing our sins, and sin will leave us powerless to see and acknowledge them, stubbornly trying to force our way ahead.

40. Unforgiveness and bitterness

Another one of those thorny issues that plagued me because of what Jesus said, just after he gave the disciples what has become known as 'The Lord's prayer': Mat 6:8 Therefore do not be like them, for your Father knows what things you have need of, before you ask Him. :9 Therefore pray in this way: Our Father, who is in Heaven, Hallowed be Your name. :10 Your kingdom come, Your will be done, on earth as it is in Heaven. :11 Give us this day our daily bread; :12 and forgive us our debts as we also forgive our debtors. :13 And lead us not into temptation, but deliver us from the evil. For Yours is the kingdom, and the power, and the glory, forever. Amen.
:14 For if you forgive men their trespasses, your heavenly Father will also forgive you; :15 but if you do not forgive men their trespasses, neither will your Father forgive your trespasses.

As pointed out earlier, the fact that God cannot forgive me if I don't forgive others, and that God can resist me because of my pride was a double whammy to me. I had to at least try to get rid of these evils in my life. That set me on a path to get to the root, and led to this book. Believe me, I struggle with all the above to this day. Now it is only easier to identify them, and take action. The solution is not permanent because we are cracked vessels. We need to be filled up with the Spirit every day. We need to pray and take in God's word daily. We must put on the armour of God every morning ready to fight the attacks of the enemy. Eph 6:13 'Therefore take to yourselves the whole armor of God, that you may be able to withstand in the evil day, and having done all, to stand. :14 Therefore stand, having your loins girded about with truth, and having on the breastplate of righteousness :15 and your feet shod with the preparation of the gospel of peace. :16 Above all, take the shield of faith, with which you shall be able to quench all the fiery darts of the wicked. :17 And take the helmet of salvation, and the sword of the Spirit, which is the Word of God, :18 praying always with all prayer and supplication in the Spirit, and watching to this very thing with all perseverance and supplication for all saints.'

God does more than just forgive our sins when we honestly confess it, He even heals the land: 2Ch 7:14 'if My people, who are called by My name, shall humble themselves and pray, and seek My face, and turn from their wicked ways, then I will hear from Heaven and will forgive their sin and will heal their land.'

In Matthew we read a story which illustrates much of how we humans think and function. We want forgiveness and pardon, but do not give it to others. God gives instant forgiveness and forgets about it: Heb 8:12 'For I will be merciful to their unrighteousness, and their sins and their iniquities I will remember no more.'

This story in Matthew describes a servant who was pardoned but then took revenge on someone who was guilty of the same crime he was.
Mat 18:23 'Therefore the kingdom of Heaven has been compared to a certain king who desired to make an accounting with his servants. :24 And when he had begun to count, one was brought to him who owed him ten thousand talents. :25 But as he had nothing to pay, his lord commanded that he, and his wife and children, and all that he had, be sold, and payment be made. :26 Then the servant fell down and worshiped him, saying, Lord, have patience with me and I will pay you all.
:27 Then the lord of that servant was moved with compassion and released him and forgave him the debt. :28 But the same servant went out and found one of his fellow servants who owed him a hundred denarii. And he laid hands on him and took him by the throat, saying, Pay me what you owe. :29 And his fellow servant fell down at his feet and begged him, saying, Have patience with me and I will pay you all. :30 And he would not, but went and cast him into prison until he should pay the debt. :31 So when his fellow servants saw what was done, they were very sorry. And they came and told their lord all that was done. :32 Then his lord, after he had called him, said to him, O wicked servant, I forgave you all that debt because you begged me. :33 Should you not also have pitied your fellow servant, even as I had pity on you? :34 And his lord was angry, and delivered him to the tormentors until he should pay all that was due to him. :35 So likewise shall My heavenly

Father do also to you, unless each one of you from your hearts forgive his brother their trespasses.'

Unforgiveness leads to bitterness and that leads to all kinds of evil and even sickness.
Act 8:23 'For I see that you are in the gall of bitterness and in the bond of iniquity.'
Eph 4:31 'Let all bitterness and wrath and anger and tumult and evil speaking be put away from you, with all malice.'
Heb 12:14 'Follow peace with all, and holiness, without which no one shall see the Lord; :15 looking diligently lest any fail of the grace of God, or lest any root of bitterness springing up disturb you, and by it many are defiled.'
Here Paul is saying that we, as well as others are defiled by bitterness. The perfect example of forgiveness came from our Saviour Jesus Christ on the cross when He was crucified. Refusing to be revengeful and bitter, He forgave: Luk 23:34 'And Jesus said, Father, forgive them, for they do not know what they do. And parting His clothing, they cast lots.'

One who followed the example of Jesus when it comes to forgiveness was Stephen, who fearlessly proclaimed the gospel of Jesus and paid the ultimate price by being stoned: Act 7:54 'And hearing these things, they were cut to their hearts. And they gnashed on him with their teeth. :55 But being full of the Holy Spirit, looking up intently into Heaven, he saw the glory of God, and Jesus standing at the right hand of God. :56 And he said, Behold, I see Heaven opened and the Son of Man standing on the right hand of God. :57 And crying out with a loud voice, they stopped their ears and ran on him with one accord. :58 And throwing him outside the city, they stoned him. And the witnesses laid their clothes down at the feet of a young man named Saul. :59 And they stoned Stephen, who was calling on God and saying, Lord Jesus, receive my spirit. :60 And kneeling down, he cried with a loud voice, Lord, do not lay this sin to their charge. And when he had said this, he fell asleep.'

What is remarkable here is that Stephen saw Jesus *standing* next to God. Scripture teaches us that He *sits* at the right hand of God. We have to see this in the context of the Roman times during the early church. When a ruler stood up, it was usually to give a judgement. His Lord and Saviour was standing up to wipe out these murderers that were stoning him. Stephen saw it but plead for their forgiveness. What a fine example by this saint. Oh God, help us to be faithful even in the face of death.

Saul, who later became Paul (the scholarly and fiery evangelist) stood by watching Stephen get stoned: Act 22:20 'And when the blood of Your martyr Stephen was poured out, I also was standing by and consenting to his death, and holding the garments of those who killed him.' Paul actively persecuted Christians when he was still a staunch Pharisee, until he met the Lord on the road to Damascus.

41. Ungratefulness

Paul writes to Timothy where he talks about being 'unthankful' and puts it on the same level with a whole lot of other evils: 2Ti 3:1 'Know this also, that in the last days grievous times will be at hand. :2 For men will be self-lovers, money-lovers, boasters, proud, blasphemers, disobedient to parents, unthankful, unholy, :3 without natural affection, unyielding, false accusers, without self-control, savage, despisers of good, :4 traitors, reckless, puffed up, lovers of pleasure rather than lovers of God,
:5 having a form of godliness, but denying the power of it; even turn away from these.'

While the Israelites wandered in the desert, they became grumpy, dissatisfied and ungrateful for the manna they received: Num 11:4 'And the mixed multitude in their midst lusted with great lust. And the sons of Israel also turned and wept, and said, Who shall give us flesh to eat? :5 We remember the fish which we ate freely in Egypt, the cucumbers, and the melons, and the leeks, and the onions, and the garlic. :6 But now our soul is dried away; there is nothing at all besides this manna before our eyes.'
They were longing back to Egypt. We know that Egypt represents our past sinful life. A life of slavery and bondage.
Are we really thankful for the Word of God? For what Jesus did on the cross? For the wife and family, he gave me? For the employment he gave me? For the talents he gave me? For what I already possess in terms of earthly possessions? For the parents he gave me? To be honest, we fail

in many of these areas leaving us vulnerable for all kinds of evil influences.

James urges us to be patient in times of testing and actually consider it good, and be grateful about it. Think of an athlete who has a tough and demanding coach. He might often be grumpy and unthankful about this person, but when he stands on the podium with a cup in his hand, he understands and will be grateful that the coach drove him hard. His sacrifices now paid off. Jas 1:2 'My brothers, count it all joy when you fall into different kinds of temptations, :3 knowing that the trying of your faith works patience. :4 But let patience have its perfect work, so that you may be perfect and entire, lacking nothing. :5 But if any of you lacks wisdom, let him ask of God, who gives to all liberally and with no reproach, and it shall be given to him.'

42.   Unteachable spirit

It was when I started teaching English in Taiwan when this spirit was exposed in me. It was the first time someone used this term and she was talking to, and about me.

My education and background weren't teaching but I hold degrees in Social Sciences and Library Science and I was teaching English as a foreign / second language. I had a friend who was already teaching in Taiwan for a more than a year. She arranged a job for me at the same school she was teaching at. She was trained as a teacher and had many years' experience. There was a lot that I could learn from her. I observed some of her classes so I could get a feel for the job, and also to learn from her. After a while, she started observing

me and gave me tips and advice which I, Mr. Proudful would not follow because I knew better. She eventually got fed-up with it, and told me I had an unteachable spirit.
Somehow it bothered me, because I realized it was true, but I could not lay my finger on the root. It was later when I realized that it is only pride, more pride and detestable pride.
This spirit is rife, not only amongst Christians, but also working very actively in Asia where I'm living now and writing this book.
The landlord (Asian) I'm renting a cabin from has an incredible controlling spirit, coupled with an unteachable spirit. These two spirits seem to work together quite often. This is a clear indication that it does not know any boundaries and cuts across cultures, languages, races and religions. I stopped giving him advice in areas where I can clearly see he has no clue because I know, he will simply do it his way until he realizes it doesn't work.
Thankfully, I don't think God ever gives up on us, but other people do. This could lead to other people ignoring and avoiding us because they know our attitude, and in the process, we might be losing out on wonderful opportunities in business and relationships.
Is it really helpful in hearing from God, and even if we do hear from Him, will we obey? Can you see the dilemma? We wouldn't follow God's plan for our life because of our pride, but will rather follow our own way.
We must become disciples of Christ. Some churches have discipling schools where new converts are trained and taught what it means to follow Jesus. If you have an unteachable spirit,

how will you learn? How will you learn and obey the Word of God?
A disciple is a follower. You can't follow if you're rebellious and unteachable.
Jesus gave this command before he ascended into heaven: Mat 28:18 'And Jesus came and spoke to them, saying, All authority is given to Me in Heaven and in earth. :19 Therefore go and teach all nations, baptizing them in the name of the Father and of the Son and of the Holy Spirit, :20 teaching them to observe all things, whatever I commanded you. And, behold, I am with you all the days until the end of the world. Amen.'

When this spirit is active in us, we become defensive. That is the trick of the enemy. You feel that by arguing and 'discussing' the matter, you are actually open to move away from your point of view, but all you're doing is really defending and justifying yourself.
I know somebody, who does the exact opposite. Listening carefully and agreeing with you, but then goes and does the opposite because of this unteachable spirit.
Good examples in the Bible of this spirit were the Pharisees. They thought they knew everything and had everything covered, always trying to corner Jesus with clever arguments thinking they knew everything there was to know about spiritual matters.
Jesus got fed-up with their knit-picking arguments and told them this: Joh 8:41 'You do the deeds of your father. Then they said to Him, We are not born of fornication; we have one father, even God. :42 Jesus said to them, If God were your father, you would love Me, for I went forth and came from

God; for I did not come of Myself, but He sent Me. :43 Why do you not know My speech? Because you cannot hear My Word. :44 You are of the Devil as father, and the lusts of your father you will do. He was a murderer from the beginning, and did not abide in the truth because there is no truth in him. When he speaks a lie, he speaks of his own, for he is a liar and the father of it.'

Proverbs encourages us to have a teachable spirit: Pro 13:18 'Poverty and shame shall be to him who refuses instruction, but he who listens to correction shall be honored.'

Pro 12:1 'Whoever loves instruction loves knowledge; but he who hates correction is like a brute animal.'

Job had a teachable spirit. He constantly asked God to teach him: Job 33:33 'If not, listen to me; be silent, and I will teach you wisdom.'

Job 34:32 'Besides what I see, You teach me; if I have done iniquity, I will do it no more.'

The Psalmist also begged for instruction and teaching: Psa 25:4 'Make me know Your ways, O Jehovah; teach me Your paths. :5 Lead me in Your truth, and teach me; for You are the God of my salvation; on You I wait all the day long.'

Psa 119:66 'Teach me good judgment and knowledge; for I have believed Your commandments.'

Psa 143:10 'Teach me to do Your will; for You are my God; Your Spirit is good; lead me into the land of uprightness.'

43. The Slumbering spirit

This spirit is so common in the church. We go to church, listen to a powerful sermon, but it all seems to fly over our heads. We sit there with eyes wide open but not absorbing anything. You can get a married couple, both reborn, baptized, spirit-filled Christians – they hear the music, but they can't dance together – figuratively speaking. If they dance, they are out of step and trample on each other's toes.

John and Paula Sandford described this spirit very well in their book 'Healing the wounded spirit'.

It often works like someone playing the guitar well, but when they sing, they are out of tune. There is no flow. There's a blockage.

Isa 56:10 'His watchmen are blind; they are all ignorant; they are all dumb dogs who cannot bark, dreaming, lying down, loving to slumber.'
When we're a reborn child of the Living God, we get a spirit of life, a quickening spirit as some Bible versions say. When God himself comes to live in us, and He does not slumber or sleep. Psa 121:3 'He will not allow your foot to be moved; He who keeps you will not slumber. :4 Behold, He who keeps Israel shall neither slumber nor sleep.'
The slumbering Christian is the one who knows the truth, but can't help himself sinning in one or more areas. Some might have a 'get quick rich' mentality and would go to a gambling den, believing that they are going to win big and get out of financial debt, meanwhile losing and squandering their last bit of money while their families suffer. They just can't get out of a cycle. An unfaithful spouse who keeps on falling into the

same trap time and again. Well aware that they are sinning but just can't break the cycle.

I have found myself in this pattern and cycle. This often occurs when we stop praying: 1Ch 16:11 'Seek Jehovah and His strength; seek His face continually.' 1Th 5:17 'Pray without ceasing.'

When we don't get fed by God's word every day: Eph 5:26 'that He might sanctify and cleanse it with the washing of water by the Word,' – we don't get washed.

When we stop meeting and having communion with fellow believers: Heb 10:25 'not forsaking the assembling of ourselves together, as the manner of some is, but exhorting one another, and so much the more as you see the Day approaching.'

Things that can wound the personal spirit are: rejection (in the womb and emotionally later in life), verbal and physical abuse, abandonment and loneliness, joblessness, traumas and sickness we might have endured, can cause a person to open up to the slumbering spirit. To get away from all the painful thoughts, we can start to retract into a fantasy world. In this world things are better and we feel safe. A world where we think we are in the presence of God, but actually fooled by the devil. To overcome the slumbering spirit, our personal spirit must be connected to the Holy Spirit. One would think that it is automatic. There are some denominations where being baptized by the Holy Spirit is frowned upon leaving fertile soul for the slumbering spirit to grow. I believe that as soon as someone is converted and accepts Jesus Christ as his personal saviour, that they should be baptized as soon as possible with the laying on of hands.

When Philip saw an eunuch from Ethiopia reading scripture, he went to the man and asked him if he understood what he read. The eunuch asked for a deeper explanation and Philip explained to him the gospel of Jesus. The man accepted Jesus. Act 8:35 'Then Philip opened his mouth and began at the same Scripture and preached the gospel of Jesus to him. :36 And as they passed along the way, they came on some water. And the eunuch said, See, here is water, what hinders me from being baptized? :37 Philip said, If you believe with all your heart, it is lawful. And he answered and said, I believe that Jesus Christ is the Son of God. :38 And he commanded the chariot to stand still. And they both went down into the water, both Philip and the eunuch. And he baptized him.'

Act 8:14 'And the apostles in Jerusalem hearing that Samaria had received the Word of God, they sent Peter and John to them; :15 who when they had come down, prayed for them that they might receive the Holy Spirit. :16 For as yet He had not fallen on any of them, they were baptized only in the name of the Lord Jesus. :17 Then they laid their hands on them, and they received the Holy Spirit. :18 And when Simon saw that the Holy Spirit was given through laying on of the apostles' hands, he offered them money,'

Here we can see that the Holy Spirit is received after conversion, then baptism and then the laying on of hands.

Once we received it, we stay in contact with Holy Spirit power via prayer, communion, assembly with the saints and reading the Word of God.

When our personal spirit connects with the Holy Spirit, our spirit comes alive and is quickened. People with a quickened spirit will always look for solutions, come up with creative ideas to solve problems while the slumbering spirit falls into depression and darkness. The alive spirit reads the Word of God and some passages in the Bible just leaps out and brings revelation. Peels are removed from the eyes and there is clarity and purpose.

The Holy Spirit flows through the quickened spirit so it can be of service to the body of Christ through prophesy, revealing roots of sickness, breaking spirits of division amongst Christians, counselling, interpreting tongues and much more. Jesus promised this: Joh 7:38 'He who believes on Me, as the Scripture has said, "Out of his belly shall flow rivers of living water." :39 (But He spoke this about the Spirit, which they who believed on Him should receive; for the Holy Spirit was not yet given, because Jesus was not yet glorified.)'

Yes, the flowing Living water will wash us clean and there will be a constant flow through us to bless and council others.

The path and process to get rid of Pride is Humility. According to Scripture, there is no other route than Humility. It is the only antidote to the scourge of Pride. I could find no better explanation of Humility than expressed by Andrew Murray. Here is a book that can be downloaded for free of the Internet about Humility.

I edited as little as possible without trying to change the meaning at all.

Humility

by Andrew Murray

Chapter 1

Humility: The Glory of the Creature

"They shall cast their crowns before the throne, so saying: Worthy art Thou, our Lord and our God, to receive the glory, and the honor and the power: for Thou didst create all things, and because of Thy will they are, and were created." - Rev. 4:11

When God created the universe, it was with the one object of making the creature partaker of His perfection and blessedness, and so showing forth in it the glory of His love and wisdom and power. God wished to reveal Himself in and through created beings by communicating to them as much of His own goodness and glory as they were capable of receiving. But this communication was not a giving to the creature something which it could possess in itself, a certain life or goodness, of which it had the charge and disposal. By no means. But as God is the ever-living, ever-present, ever-acting One, who upholds all things by the word of His power, and in whom all things exist, the relation of the creature to God could only be one of unceasing, absolute, universal dependence. As truly as God by His power once created, so truly by that same power must God every moment maintain. The creature has not only to look back to the origin and first beginning of existence, and acknowledge that it there owes everything to God; its chief care, its highest virtue, its only happiness, now and through all eternity, is to present itself an empty vessel, in which God can dwell and manifest His power and goodness. The life God bestows is imparted not once and for all, but each moment continuously, by the unceasing operation of His mighty power. Humility, the place of entire dependence on God, is, from the very nature of things, the first duty and the highest virtue of the creature, and the root of every virtue.

And so pride, or the loss of this humility, is the root of every sin and evil. It was when the now fallen angels began to look upon themselves with self-complacency that they were led to disobedience, and were cast down from the light of heaven into outer darkness. Even so it was, when the serpent breathed the poison of his pride, the desire to be as God, into the hearts of our first parents, that they too fell from their high estate into all the wretchedness in which man is now sunk. In heaven and earth, pride, self-exaltation, is the gate and the birth, and the curse, of hell. [1]

Hence it follows that nothing can be our redemption, but the restoration of the lost humility, the original and only true relation of the creature to its God. And so Jesus came to bring humility back to earth, to make us partakers of it, and by it to save us. In heaven He humbled Himself to become man. The humility we see in Him possessed Him in heaven; it brought Him, He brought it, from there. Here on earth "He humbled Himself, and became obedient unto death"; His humility gave His death its value, and so became our redemption. And now the salvation He imparts is nothing less and nothing else than a communication of His own life and death, His own disposition and spirit, His own humility, as the ground and root of His relation to God and His redeeming work. Jesus Christ took the place and fulfilled the destiny of man, as a creature, by His life of perfect humility. His humility is our salvation. His salvation is our humility.

And so the life of the saved ones, of the saints, must bear this stamp of deliverance from sin, and full restoration to their original state; their whole relation to God and man marked by an all-pervading humility. Without this there can be no true abiding in God's presence, or experience of His favor and the power of His Spirit; without this no abiding faith, or love or joy or strength. Humility is the only soil in which the graces root; the lack of humility is the sufficient explanation of every defect and failure. Humility is not so much a grace or virtue along with others; it is the root of all, because it alone takes the right attitude before God, and allows Him as God to do all.

God has so constituted us as reasonable beings, that the truer the insight into the real nature or the absolute need of a command, the readier and fuller will be our obedience to it. The call to humility has been too little regarded in the Church because its true nature and importance has been too little apprehended. It is not something which we bring to God, or He bestows; it is simply the sense of entire nothingness, which comes when we see how truly God is all, and in which we make way for God to be all. When the creature realizes that this is the true nobility, and consents to be with his will, his mind, and his affections, the form, the vessel in which the life and glory of God are to work and manifest themselves, he sees that humility is simply acknowledging the truth of his position as creature, and yielding to God His place.

In the life of earnest Christians, of those who pursue and profess holiness, humility ought to be the chief mark of their uprightness. It is often said that it is not so. May not one reason be that in the teaching and example of the Church, it has never had that place of supreme importance which belongs to it? And that this, again, is owing to the neglect of this truth, that strong as sin is as a motive to humility, there is one of still wider and mightier influence, that which makes the angels, that which made Jesus, that which makes the holiest of saints in heaven, so humble; that the first and chief mark of the relation of the creature, the secret of his blessedness, is the humility and nothingness which leaves God free to be all?

I am sure there are many Christians who will confess that their experience has been very much like my own in this, that we had long known the Lord without realizing that meekness and lowliness of heart are to be the distinguishing feature of the disciple as they were of the Master. And further, that this humility is not a thing that will come of itself, but that it must be made the object of special desire and prayer and faith and practice. As we study the word, we shall see what very distinct and oft-repeated instructions Jesus gave His disciples on this point, and how slow they were in understanding Him. Let us, at the very commencement of our meditations, admit that there is nothing so natural to man, nothing so insidious and hidden from our sight, nothing so difficult and dangerous, as pride. Let us feel that nothing but a very determined and persevering waiting on God and Christ will discover how lacking we are in the grace of humility, and how impotent to obtain what we seek. Let us study the character of Christ until our souls are filled with the love and admiration of His lowliness. And let us believe that, when we are broken down under a sense of our pride, and our impotence to cast it out, Jesus Christ Himself will come in to impart this grace too, as a part of His wondrous life within us.

Chapter 2

Humility: The Secret of Redemption

"Have this mind in you which was also in Christ Jesus: who emptied Himself; taking the form of a servant; and humbled Himself; becoming obedient even unto death. Wherefore God also highly exalted Him. "Phil. 2:5-9.

No tree can grow except on the root from which it sprang. Through all its existence it can only live with the life that was in the seed that gave it being. The full apprehension of this truth in its application to the first and the Second Adam cannot but help us greatly to understand both the need and the nature of the redemption there is in Jesus.
The Need. -- When the Old Serpent, he who had been cast out from heaven for his pride, whose whole nature as devil was pride, spoke his words of temptation into the ear of Eve, these words carried with them the very poison of hell. And when she listened, and yielded her desire and her

will to the prospect of being as God, knowing good and evil, the poison entered into her soul and blood and life, destroying forever that blessed humility and dependence upon God which would have been our everlasting happiness. And instead of this, her life and the life of the race that sprang from her became corrupted to its very root with that most terrible of all sins and all curses, the poison of Satan's own pride. All the wretchedness of which this world has been the scene, all its wars and bloodshed among the nations, all its selfishness and suffering, all its ambitions and jealousies, all its broken hearts and embittered lives, with all its daily unhappiness, have their origin in what this cursed, hellish pride, either our own, or that of others, has brought us. It is pride that made redemption needful; it is from our pride we need above everything to be redeemed. And our insight into the need of redemption will largely depend upon our knowledge of the terrible nature of the power that has entered our being.

No tree can grow except on the root from which it sprang. The power that Satan brought from hell, and cast into man's life, is working daily, hourly, with mighty power throughout the world. Men suffer from it; they fear and fight and flee it; and yet they know not where it comes, where it has its terrible supremacy. No wonder they do not know where or how it is to be overcome. Pride has its root and strength in a terrible spiritual power, outside of us as well as within us; as needful as it is that we confess and deplore it as our very own, is to know it in its Satanic origin. If this leads us to utter despair of ever conquering or casting it out, it will lead us all the sooner to that supernatural power in which alone our deliverance is to be found; the redemption of the Lamb of God. The hopeless struggle against the workings of self and pride within us may indeed become still more hopeless as we think of the power of darkness behind it all; the utter despair will fit us the better for realizing and accepting a power and a life outside of ourselves too, even the humility of heaven as brought down and brought near by the Lamb of God, to cast out Satan and his pride.

No tree can grow except on the root from which it sprang. Even as we need to look to the first Adam and his fall to know the power of the sin within us, we need to know well the Second Adam and His power to give within us a life of humility as real and abiding and overmastering as has been that of pride. We have our life from and in Christ, as truly, yea more truly, than from and in Adam. We are to walk "rooted in Him," "holding fast the Head from whom the whole body increases with the increase of God." The life of God, which in the incarnation entered human nature, is the root in which we are to stand and grow; it is the same almighty power that worked there and then onward to the resurrection, which works daily in us. Our one need is to study and know and trust the life that has been revealed in Christ as the life that is now ours, and waits for our consent to gain possession and mastery of our whole being.

In this view it is of inconceivable importance that we should have right thoughts of what Christ is, of what really constitutes Him the Christ, and specially of what may be counted His chief characteristic, the root and essence of all His character as our Redeemer. There can be but one answer: it is His humility. What is the incarnation but His heavenly humility, His emptying Himself and becoming man? What is His life on earth but humility; His taking the form of a servant? And what is His atonement but humility? "He humbled Himself and became obedient unto death." And what is His ascension and His glory, but humility exalted to the throne and crowned with glory? He humbled Himself, therefore God highly exalted Him." In heaven, where He was with the Father, in His birth, in His life, in His death, in His sitting on the throne, it is nothing but humility. Christ is the humility of God embodied in human nature; the Eternal Love humbling itself, clothing itself in the clothes of meekness and gentleness, to win and serve and save us. As the love and condescension of God makes Him the benefactor and helper and servant of all, so Jesus of necessity was the Incarnate Humility. And so He is still in the midst of the throne, the meek and lowly Lamb of God.

If this be the root of the tree, its nature must be seen in every branch and leaf and fruit. If humility be the first, the all-including grace of the life of Jesus,--if humility be the secret of His atonement, then the health and strength of our spiritual life will entirely depend upon our putting this grace first too, and making humility the chief thing we admire in Him, the chief thing we ask of Him, the one thing for which we sacrifice all else. [2]

Is it any wonder that the Christian life is so often feeble and fruitless, when the very root of the Christ life is neglected, is unknown? Is it any wonder that the joy of salvation is so little felt, when that in which Christ found it and brings it, is so little sought? Until a humility which will rest in nothing less than the end and death of self; which gives up all the honor of men as Jesus did, to seek the honor that comes from God alone; which absolutely makes and counts itself nothing, that God may be all, that the Lord alone may be exalted, --until such a humility be what we seek in Christ above our chief joy, and welcome at any price, there is very little hope of a religion that will conquer the world.

I cannot too earnestly plead with my reader, if possibly his attention has never yet been specially directed to the want there is of humility within him or around him, to pause and ask whether he sees much of the spirit of the meek and lowly Lamb of God in those who are called by His name. Let him consider how all want of love, all indifference to the needs, the feelings, the weakness of others; all sharp and hasty judgments and utterances, so often excused under the plea of being outright and honest; all manifestations of temper and touchiness and irritation; all feelings of bitterness and estrangement, have their root in nothing but pride, that ever seeks itself, and his eyes will be opened to see how a dark, shall I not say a devilish pride, creeps in almost everywhere, the assemblies of the saints not excepted. Let him begin to ask what would be the effect, if in himself and around him, if towards fellow-saints and the world, believers were really permanently guided by the humility of Jesus; and let him say if the cry of our whole heart, night and day, ought not to be, Oh for the humility of Jesus in myself and all around me! Let him honestly fix his heart on his own lack of the humility which has been revealed in the likeness of Christ's life, and in the whole character of His redemption, and he will begin to feel as if he had never yet really known what Christ and His salvation is.

Believer, study the humility of Jesus. This is the secret, the hidden root of your redemption. Sink down into it deeper day by day. Believe with your whole heart that this Christ, whom God has given thee, even as His divine humility wrought the work for thee, will enter in to dwell and work within you too, and make you what the Father would have you to be.

Chapter 3

Humility in the Life of Jesus

"I am in the midst of you as he that serveth." Luke 22: 27

In the Gospel of John, we have the inner life of our Lord laid open to us. Jesus speaks frequently of His relation to the Father, of the motives by which He is guided, of His consciousness of the power and spirit in which He acts. Though the word humble does not occur, we shall nowhere in Scripture see so clearly wherein His humility consisted. We have already said that this grace is in truth nothing but that simple consent of the creature to let God be all, in virtue of which it surrenders itself to His working alone. In Jesus we shall see how both as the Son of God in heaven, and as man upon earth, He took the place of entire subordination, and gave God the honor and the glory which is due to Him-- And what He taught so often was made true to Himself: "He that humbleth him: shall be exalted." As it is written,

"He humbled Himself, therefore God highly exalted Him."

Listen to the words in which our Lord speaks of His relation to the Father, and how unceasingly He uses the words not, and nothing, of Himself. The not I, in which Paul expresses his relation to Christ, is the very spirit of what Christ says of His relation the Father. "The Son can do nothing of Himself" (John 5: 19) "I can of My own self do nothing; My judgment is just, because I seek not Mine own will" (John 5: 30) "I receive not glory from men" (John 5: 41) "I am come not to do Mine own will" (John 6:38) "My teaching is not Mine" (John 7:16) "I am not come of Myself" (John 7:28) "I do nothing of Myself" (John 8:28) "I have not come of Myself, but He sent Me" (John 8: 42). "I seek not Mine own glory" (John 8:50) "The words that I say, I speak not from Myself" (John 14: 10). "The word which ye hear is not Mine" (John 14: 24).

These words open to us the deepest roots of Christ's life and work. They tell us how it was that the Almighty God was able to work His mighty redemptive work through Him. They show what Christ counted the state of heart which became Him as the Son of the Father. They teach us what the essential nature and life is of that redemption which Christ accomplished and now communicates. It is this: He was nothing, that God might be all. He resigned Himself with His will and His powers entirely for the Father to work in Him. Of His own power, His own will, and His own glory, of His whole mission with all His works and His teaching, of all this He said, It is not I; I am nothing; I have given Myself to the Father to work; I am nothing, the Father is all.

This life of entire self-denial, of absolute submission and dependence upon the Father's will, Christ found to be one of perfect peace and joy. He lost nothing by giving all to God. God honored His trust, and did all for Him, and then exalted Him to His own right hand in glory. And because Christ had thus humbled Himself before God and God was ever before Him, He found it possible to humble Himself before men too, and to be
the Servant of all. His humility was simply the surrender of Himself to God, to allow Him to do in Him what He pleased, whatever men around might say of Him, or do to Him.
It is in this state of mind, in this spirit and disposition, that the redemption of Christ has its virtue and efficacy.
It is to bring us to this disposition that we are made partakers of Christ. This is the true self-denial to which our Savior calls us, the acknowledgment that self has nothing good in it, except as an empty vessel which God must fill, and that its claim to be or do anything may not for a moment be allowed. It is in this, above and before everything, in which the conformity to Jesus consists, the being and doing nothing of ourselves, that
God may be all.
Here we have the root and nature of true humility. It is because this is not understood or sought after, that our humility is so superficial and so feeble. We must learn of Jesus, how He is meek and lowly of heart. He teaches us where true humility takes its rise and finds its strength--in the knowledge that it is God who works all in all, that our place is to yield to Him in perfect resignation

and dependence, in full consent to be and to do nothing of ourselves. This is the life Christ came to reveal and to impart--a life to God that came through death to sin and self. If we feel that this life is too high for us and beyond our reach, it must move us to seek it in Him; it is the indwelling Christ who will live in us this life, meek and lowly. If we long for this, let us, meantime, above everything, seek the holy secret of the knowledge of the nature of God, as He every moment works all in all; the secret, of which all nature and every creature, and above all, every child of God, is to be the witness,--that it is nothing but a vessel, a channel, through which the living God can manifest the riches of His wisdom, power, and goodness. The root of all virtue and grace, of all faith and acceptable worship, is that we know that we have nothing but what we receive, and bow in deepest humility to wait upon God for it.

It was because this humility was not only a temporary sentiment, wakened up and brought into exercise when He thought of God, but the very spirit of His whole life, that Jesus was just as humble in His actions with men as with God. He felt Himself the Servant of God for the men whom God made and loved; as a natural consequence, He counted Himself the Servant of men that through Him God might do His work of love. He never for a moment thought of seeking His honor, or asserting His power to vindicate Himself. His whole spirit was that of a life yielded to God to work in. It is not until Christians study the humility of Jesus as the very essence of His redemption, as the very blessedness of the life of the Son of God, as the only true relation to the Father, and therefore as that which Jesus must give us, if we are to have any part with Him, that the terrible lack of actual, heavenly, manifest humility will become a burden and a sorrow, and our ordinary religion be set aside to secure this, the first and the chief of the marks of the Christ within us.

Brother, are you clothed with humility? Ask your daily life. Ask Jesus. Ask your friends. Ask the world. And begin to praise God that there is opened up to you in Jesus, a heavenly humility of which you have hardly known, and through which a heavenly blessedness you possibly have never yet tasted can come in to you.

Chapter 4

Humility in the Teaching of Jesus

"Learn of Me, for I am meek and lowly of heart."-- Matt.11:29.
'And whoever desires to be chief among you, let him be your servant; even as the Son of Man did not come to be served, but to serve, and to give His life a ransom for many.' Matt 20: 27-28

 We have seen humility in the life of Christ, as He laid open His heart to us: let us listen to His teaching. There we shall hear how He speaks of it, and how far He expects men, and specially His disciples, to be humble as He was. Let us carefully study the passages, to receive the full impression of how often and how earnestly He taught it: it may help us to realize what He asks of us.

1. Look at the commencement of His ministry. In the Beatitudes with which the Sermon on the Mount opens, He speaks: "Blessed are the poor in spirit; for theirs is the kingdom of heaven. Blessed

are the meek; for they shall inherit the earth." The very first words of His proclamation of the kingdom of heaven reveal the open gate through which alone we enter. The poor, who have nothing in themselves, to them the kingdom comes.

The meek, who seek nothing in themselves, theirs the earth shall be. The blessings of heaven and earth are for the lowly. For the heavenly and the earthly life, humility is the secret of blessing.

2. "Learn of Me; for I am meek and lowly of heart, and ye shall find rest for your souls. "Jesus offers Himself as Teacher. He tells what the spirit both is, which we shall find Him as Teacher, and which we can learn and receive from Him. Meekness and lowliness, the one thing He offers us; in it we shall find perfect rest for our soul. Humility is to be a salvation.

3. The disciples had been disputing who would be the greatest in the kingdom, and had agreed to ask the Master (Luke 9:46; Matt. 18:3). He set a child in their midst and said, "Whosoever shall humble himself as this little child, shall be exalted." "Who is the greatest in the kingdom of heaven?" The question is indeed a far-reaching one. What will be the chief distinction in the heavenly kingdom? The answer, none but Jesus would have given. The chief glory of heaven, the true heavenly-mindedness, the chief of the graces, is humility. "He that is least among you, the same shall be great."

4. The sons of Zebedee had asked Jesus to sit on His right and left, the highest place in the kingdom. Jesus said it was not His to give, but the Father's, who would give it to those for whom it was prepared. They must not look or ask for it. Their thought must be of the cup and the baptism of

humiliation. And then He added, "Whosoever will be chief among you, let him be your servant. Even as the Son of Man came to serve." Humility, as it is the mark of Christ the heavenly, will be the one standard of glory in heaven: the lowliest is the nearest to God. The primacy in the Church is promised to the humblest.

5. Speaking to the multitude and the disciples, of the Pharisees and their love of the chief seats, Christ said once again (Matt. 23:11), "He that is greatest among you shall be your servant." Humiliation is the only ladder to honor in God's kingdom.

6. On another occasion, in the house of a Pharisee, He spoke the parable of the guest who would be invited to come up higher (Luke 14:1-11), and added, "For whosoever exalteth himself shall be abased; and he that humbleth himself shall be exalted." The demand is unchangeable; there is no other way. Self-abasement alone will be exalted.

7. After the parable of the Pharisee and the Publican, Christ spoke again (Luke18: 14), "Everyone that exalteth himself shall be abased; and he that humbleth himself shall be exalted." In the temple and presence and worship of God, everything is worthless that is not pervaded by deep, true humility towards God and men.

8. After washing the disciples' feet, Jesus said (John 13:14), "If I then, the Lord and Master, have washed your feet, ye also ought to wash one another's feet." The authority of command, and example, every thought, either of obedience or conformity, make humility the first and most essential element of discipleship.

9. At the Holy Supper table, the disciples still disputed who should be greatest (Luke 22:26). Jesus said, "He that is greatest among you, let him be as the younger; and he that is chief, as he that doth serve. I am among you as he that serveth." The path in which Jesus walked, and which He opened up for us, the power and spirit in which He wrought out salvation, and to which He saves us, is ever the humility that makes me the servant of all.

How little this is preached. How little it is practiced. How little the lack of it is felt or confessed. How few ever think, of making it a distinct object of continual desire or prayer? How little the world has seen it? How little has it been seen even in the inner circle of the Church? "Whosoever will be chief among you, let him be your servant." May God help us to believe that Jesus means this! We all know what the character of a faithful servant or slave implies. Devotion to the master's interests, thoughtful study and care to please him, delight in his prosperity and honor and happiness. There are servants on earth in whom these dispositions have been seen, and to whom the name of servant has never been anything but a glory. To how many of us has it not been a new joy in the Christian life to know that we may yield ourselves as servants, as slaves to God, and to find that His service is our highest liberty,--the liberty from sin and self? We need now to learn another lesson,--that Jesus calls us to be servants of one another, and that, as we accept it heartily, this service too will be a most blessed one, a new and fuller liberty too from sin and self. At first it may appear hard; this is only because of the pride which still counts itself something. If once we learn that to be nothing before God is the glory of the creature, the spirit of Jesus, the joy of heaven, we shall welcome with our whole heart the discipline we may have in serving even those who try to agitate us. When our own heart is set upon this, the true sanctification, we shall study each word of Jesus on self-denial with new zest, and no place will be too low, and no stooping too deep, and no service too mean or too long continued, if we may but share and prove the fellowship with Him who spoke, "I am among you as he that serveth". Brethren, here is the path to the higher life. Down, lower down! This was what Jesus ever said to the disciples who were thinking of being great in the kingdom, and of sitting on His right hand and His left. Seek not, ask not for exaltation; that is God's work. Look to it that you deny and humble yourselves, and take no place before God or man but that of servant; that is your work; let that be your one purpose and prayer. God is faithful. Just as water ever seeks and fills the lowest place, so the moment God finds the creature abased and empty, His glory and power flow in, to exalt and to bless. He that humbles himself -- that must be our one care -- shall be exalted; that is God's care; by His mighty power and in His great love He will do it.

Men sometimes speak as if humility and meekness would rob us of what is noble and bold and manlike. Oh that all would believe that this is the nobility of the kingdom of heaven, that this is the royal spirit that the King of heaven displayed, that this is Godlike, to humble oneself, to become the servant of all! This is the path to the gladness and the glory of Christ's presence ever in us, His power ever resting on us. Jesus, the meek and lowly One, calls us to learn of Him the path to God. Let us study the words we have been reading, until our heart is filled with the thought: My one need is humility. And let us believe that what He shows, He gives; what He is, He imparts. As the meek and lowly One, He will come in and dwell in the longing heart.

Chapter 5

Humility in the Disciples of Jesus

"Let him that is chief among you be as he that doth serve." --Luke 22:26.

We have studied humility in the person and teaching of Jesus; let us now look for it in the circle of His chosen companions-the twelve apostles. If, in the lack of it we find in them, the contrast between Christ and men is brought out more clearly, it will help us to appreciate the mighty change which Pentecost caused in them, and prove how real our participation can be in the perfect triumph of Christ's humility over the pride Satan had breathed into man.
In the texts quoted from the teaching of Jesus, we have already seen what the occasions were on which the disciples had proved how entirely wanting they were in the grace of humility. Once, they had been disputing the way which of them should be the greatest. Another time, the sons of Zebedee with their mother had asked for the first places--the seat on the right hand and the left. And, later on, at the Supper table on the last night, there was again a contention which should be accounted the greatest. Not that there were not

moments when they indeed humbled themselves before their Lord. So it was with Peter when he cried out, "Depart from me, Lord, for I am a sinful man." So, too, with the disciples when they fell down and worshiped Him who had stilled the storm. But such occasional expressions of humility only bring out into stronger relief what was the habitual tone of their mind, as shown in the natural and spontaneous revelation given at other times of the place and the power of self. The study of the meaning of all this will teach us very important lessons.

Firstly, How much there may be of earnest and active religion while humility is still sadly wanting? See it in the disciples. There was in them fervent attachment to Jesus. They had forsaken all for Him. The Father had revealed to them that He was the Christ of God. They believed in Him, they loved Him, they obeyed His commandments. They had forsaken all to follow Him. When others went back, they stayed with Him. They were ready to die with Him. But deeper down than all this there was a dark power, of the existence and the hideousness of which they were hardly conscious, which had to be slain and cast out, before they could be the witnesses of the power of Jesus to save. It is even so today. We may find professors and ministers, evangelists and workers, missionaries and teachers, in whom the gifts of the Spirit are many and manifest, and who are the channels of blessing to multitudes, but of whom, when the testing time comes, or closer observation gives fuller knowledge, it is only too painfully manifest that the grace of humility, as an abiding characteristic, is hardly to be seen. All tends to confirm the lesson that humility is one of the chief and the highest graces; one of the most difficult of attainment; one to which our first and highest efforts ought to be directed; one that only comes in power, when the fullness of the Spirit makes us partakers of the indwelling Christ, and He lives within us.

Secondly, How impotent all external teaching and all personal effort is, to conquer pride or give the meek a lowly heart. For three years the disciples had been in the training school of Jesus. He had told them what the chief lesson was He wished to teach them: "Learn of Me, for I am meek and lowly in heart." Time after time He had spoken to them, to the Pharisees, to the multitude, of humility as the only path to the glory of God. He had not only lived before them as the Lamb of God in His divine humility, He had more than once unfolded to them the inmost secret of His life: "The Son of Man came not to be served, but to serve"; "I am among you as one that serves." He had washed their feet, and told them they were to follow His example. And yet all had little effect. At the Holy Supper there was still the contention as to who should be greatest. They had doubtless often tried to learn His lessons, and firmly resolved not again to grieve Him. But all in vain. To teach them and us the much needed lesson, that no outward instruction, not even of Christ Himself; no argument however convincing; no sense of the beauty of humility, however deep; no personal resolve or effort, however sincere and earnest, can cast out the devil of pride. When Satan casts out Satan, it is only to enter afresh in a mightier, though more hidden power. Nothing can avail but this, that the new nature in its divine humility be

revealed in power to take the place of the old, to become as truly our very nature as that ever was. Thirdly. It is only by the indwelling of Christ in His divine humility that we become truly humble. We have our pride from another, from Adam; we must have our humility from Another too. Pride is ours, and rules in us with such terrible power, because it is ourselves, our very nature. Humility must be ours in the same way; it must be our very self, our very nature. As natural and easy as it has been to be proud, it must be, it will be, to be humble. The promise is, "Where," even in the heart, "sin abounded, grace did abound more exceedingly." All Christ's teaching of His disciples, and all their vain efforts, were the needful reparation for His entering into them in divine power, to give and be in them what He had taught them to desire. In His death He destroyed the power of the devil, He put away sin, and effected an everlasting redemption. In His resurrection He received from the Father an entirely new life, the life of man in the power of God, capable of being
communicated to men, and entering and renewing and filling their lives with His divine power. In His ascension He received the Spirit of the Father, through whom He might do what He could not do while upon earth, make Himself one with those He loved, actually live their life for them, so that they could live before the Father in a humility like His, because it was Himself who lived and breathed in them. And on Pentecost He came and took possession. The work of preparation and conviction, the awakening of desire and hope which His teaching had affected, was perfected by the mighty change that Pentecost brought. And the lives and the epistles of James and Peter and

John bear witness that all was changed, and that the spirit of the meek and suffering Jesus had indeed possession of them.

What shall we say to these things? Among my readers I am sure there is more than one class. There may be some who have never yet thought very specially of the matter, and cannot at once realize its immense importance as a life question for the Church and its every member. There are others who have felt condemned for their shortcomings, and have put forth very earnest efforts, only to fail and be discouraged. Others, again, may be able to give joyful testimony of spiritual blessing and power, and yet there has never been the needed conviction of what those around them still see as wanting. And still others may be able to witness that in regard to this grace too the Lord has given deliverance and victory, while He has taught them how much they still need and may expect out of the fullness of Jesus. To whichever class we belong, may I urge the pressing need there is for our all seeking a still deeper conviction of the unique place that humility holds in the religion of Christ, and the utter impossibility of the Church or the believer being what Christ would have them be, as long as His humility is not recognized as His chief glory, His first command, and our highest blessedness. Let us consider deeply how far the disciples were advanced while this grace was still so terribly lacking, and let us pray to God that other gifts may not so satisfy us, that we never grasp the fact that the absence of this grace is the secret cause why the power of God cannot do its mighty work. It is only where we, like the Son, truly know and show

that we can do nothing of ourselves, that God will do all.
It is when the truth of an indwelling Christ takes the place it claims in the experience of believers, that the Church will put on her beautiful garments and humility be seen in her teachers and members as the beauty of holiness.

Chapter 6

Humility in Daily Life

"He that loveth not his brother whom he hath seen, how can he love God whom he hath not seen?" 1 John 4:20.

What a solemn thought, that our love to God will be measured by our everyday dealings with men and the love it displays; and that our love to God will be found to be a delusion, except as its truth is proved in standing the test of daily life with our fellow-men. It is even so with our humility. It is easy to think we humble ourselves before God: humility towards men will be the only sufficient proof that our humility before God is real; that humility has taken up its abode in us; and become our very nature; that we actually, like Christ, have made ourselves of no reputation. When in the presence of God lowliness of heart has become, not a posture we pray to Him, but the very spirit of our life, it will manifest itself in all our behaviour towards our brethren. The lesson is one of deep importance. The only humility that is really ours is not that which we try to show before God in prayer, but that which we carry with us, and carry out, in our ordinary conduct; the insignificance of daily life are the importance and the tests of eternity, because they prove what really is the spirit that possesses us. It is in our most unguarded moments that we really show and see what we are. To know the humble man, to know how the humble man behaves, you must follow him in the common course of daily life.

Is not this what Jesus taught? It was when the disciples disputed who should be greatest; when He saw how the Pharisees loved the chief place at feasts and the chief seats in the synagogues; when He had given them the example of washing their feet,--that He taught His lessons of humility. Humility before God is nothing if not proved in humility before men.

It is even so in the teaching of Paul. To the Romans He writes: "In honor preferring one another"; "Set not your mind on high things, but condescend to those that are lowly." "Be not wise in your own conceit." To the Corinthians: "Love," and there is no love without humility as its root, "vaunteth not itself, is not puffed up, seeketh not its own, is not provoked." To the Galatians: "Through love be servants one of another. Let us not
be desirous of vainglory, provoking one another, envying one another." To the Ephesians, immediately after the three wonderful chapters on the heavenly life: "Therefore, walk with all lowliness and meekness, with long-suffering, forbearing one another in love"; "Giving thanks always, subjecting yourselves one to another in the fear of Christ." To the Philippians: "Doing nothing through faction or vainglory, but in lowliness of mind, each counting other better than himself. Have the mind in you which was also in

Christ Jesus, who emptied Himself, taking the form of a servant, and humbled Himself." And to the Colossians: "Put on a heart of compassion, kindness, humility, meekness, long-suffering, forbearing one another, and forgiving each other, even as the Lord forgave you." It is in our relation to one another, in our treatment of one another, that the true lowliness of mind and the heart of humility are to be seen. Our humility before God has no value, but as it prepares us to reveal the humility of Jesus to our fellow-men. Let us study humility in daily life in the light of these words. The humble man seeks at all times to act up to the rule, "In honor preferring one another; Servants one of another; Each counting others better than himself, Subjecting yourselves one to another." The question is often asked, how we can count others better than ourselves, when we see that they are far below us in wisdom and in holiness, in natural gifts, or in grace received. The question proves at once how little we understand what real lowliness of mind is. True humility comes when, in the light of God, we have seen ourselves to be nothing, have consented to part with and cast away self, to let God be all. The soul that has done this, and can say, so have I lost myself in finding Thee, no longer compares itself with others. It has given up forever every thought of self in God's presence; it meets its fellow-men as one who is nothing, and seeks nothing for itself; who is a servant of God, and for His sake a servant of all. A faithful servant may be wiser than the master, and yet retain the true spirit and posture of the servant. The humble man looks upon every, the feeblest and unworthiest child of God, and honors him and prefers him in honor as the son of a King. The spirit of Him who washed the disciples' feet, makes it a joy to us to be indeed the least, to be servants one of another.

The humble man feels no jealousy or envy. He can praise God when others are preferred and blessed before him. He can bear to hear others praised and himself forgotten, because in God's presence he has learnt to say with Paul, "I am nothing." He has received the spirit of Jesus, who pleased not Himself, and sought not His own honor, as the spirit of his life.

Amid what are considered the temptations to impatience and touchiness, to hard thoughts and sharp words, which come from the failings and sins of fellow-Christians, the humble man carries the oft-repeated injunction in his heart, and shows it in his life, "Forbearing one another, and forgiving one another, even as the Lord forgave you." He has learnt that in putting on the Lord Jesus he has put on the heart of compassion, kindness, humility, meekness, and long-suffering. Jesus has taken the place of self, and it is not an impossibility to forgive as Jesus forgave. His humility does not consist merely in thoughts or words of self-depreciation, but, as Paul puts it, in "a heart of humility," encompassed by compassion and kindness, meekness and longsuffering, the sweet and lowly gentleness recognized as the mark of the Lamb of God.

In striving after the higher experiences of the Christian life, the believer is often in danger of aiming at and rejoicing in what one might call the more human, the manly, virtues, such as boldness, joy, contempt of the world, zeal, self-sacrifice, even the old Stoics taught and practiced these, while the deeper and gentler, the diviner and more heavenly graces, those which Jesus first taught upon earth, because He brought them from heaven; those which are more distinctly connected with His cross and the death of self, poverty of spirit, meekness, humility, lowliness, are scarcely thought of or valued. Therefore, let us put on a heart of compassion, kindness, humility, meekness, long-suffering; and let us prove our Christlikeness, not only in our zeal for saving the lost, but before all in our interaction with the brethren, forbearing and forgiving one another, even as the Lord forgave us.

Fellow-Christians do let us study the Bible-portrait of the humble man. And let us ask our brethren, and ask the world, whether they recognize in us the likeness to the original. Let us be content with nothing less than taking each of these texts as the promise of what God will work in us, as the revelation in words of what the Spirit of Jesus will give as a birth within us. And let each failure and shortcoming simply urge us to turn humbly and meekly to the meek and lowly Lamb of God, in the assurance that where He is enthroned in the heart, His humility and gentleness will be one of the streams of living water that flow from within us.

"I knew Jesus, and He was very precious to my soul: but I found something in me that would not keep sweet and patient and kind. I did what I could to keep it down, but it was there. I besought Jesus to do something for me, and when I gave Him my will, He came to my heart, and took out all that would not be sweet, all that would not be kind, all that would not be patient, and then He shut the door." George Fox.

Once again I repeat what I have said before. I feel deeply that we have very little conception of what the Church suffers from the lack of this divine humility, the nothingness that makes room for God to prove His power. It is not long since a Christian, of a humble, loving spirit, acquainted with not a few mission stations of various societies, expressed his deep sorrow that in some cases the spirit of love and forbearance was sadly lacking. Men and women, who in Europe could each choose their own circle of friends, brought close together with others of uncongenial minds, find it hard to bear, and to love, and to keep the unity of the Spirit in the bond of peace. And those who should have been fellow-helpers of each other's joy, became a hindrance and weariness. And all for the one reason, the lack of the humility which counts itself nothing, which rejoices in becoming and being counted the least, and only seeks, like Jesus, to be the servant, the helper and comforter of others, even the lowest and unworthiest.

And whence comes it that men who have joyfully given up themselves for Christ, find it so hard to give up themselves for their brethren? Is not the blame with the Church? It has so little taught its sons that the humility of Christ is the first of the virtues, the best of all the graces and powers of the Spirit. But let us not be discouraged. Let the discovery of the lack of this grace stir us to larger expectation from God. Let us look upon every brother who tries or vexes us, as God's means of grace, God's instrument for our purification, for our exercise of the humility Jesus our Life breathes within us. And let us have such faith in the All of God, and the nothing of self, that, as nothing in our own eyes, we may, in God's power, only seek to serve one another in love.

Chapter 7

Humility and Holiness

"Which say, Stand by thyself... for I am holier than thou." Isaiah 65: 5

We speak of the Holiness movement in our times, and praise God for it. We hear a great deal of seekers after holiness and professors of holiness, of holiness teaching and holiness meetings. The blessed truths of holiness in Christ, and holiness by faith, are being emphasized as never before. The great test of whether the holiness we profess to seek or to attain, is truth and life, will be whether it be manifest in the increasing humility it produces. In the creature, humility is the one thing needed to allow God's holiness to dwell in him and shine through him. In Jesus, the Holy One of God who makes us holy, a divine humility was the secret of His life and His death and His exaltation; the one infallible test of our holiness will be the humility before God and men which marks us. Humility is the bloom and the beauty of holiness. The chief mark of counterfeit holiness is its lack of humility. Every seeker after holiness needs to be on his guard, lest unconsciously what was begun in the spirit be perfected in the flesh, and pride creep in where its presence is least expected. Two men went up into the temple to pray: the one a Pharisee, the other a publican. There is no place or position so sacred but the Pharisee can enter there. Pride can lift its head in the very temple of God, and make His worship the scene of its self-exaltation. Since the time Christ so exposed his pride, the Pharisee has put on the clothes of the publican, and the confessor of deep sinfulness equally with the professor of the highest holiness, must be on the watch. Just when we are most anxious to have our heart the temple of God, we shall find the two men coming up to pray. And the publican will find that his danger is not from the Pharisee beside him, who despises him, but the Pharisee within who commends and exalts. In God's temple, when we think we are in the holiest of all, in the presence of His holiness, let us be beware of pride.

"Now there was a day when the sons of God came to present themselves before the Lord, and Satan came also among them." "God, I thank thee, I am not as the rest of men, or even as this publican." It is in that which is just cause for thanksgiving, it is in the very thanksgiving which we render to God, it may be in the very confession that God has done it all, that self finds its cause of complacency. Yes, even when in the temple the language of humiliation and trust in God's mercy alone is heard, the Pharisee may take up the note of praise, and in thanking God be congratulating himself. Pride can clothe itself in the garments of praise or of humility. Even though the words, "I am not as the rest of men" are rejected and condemned, their spirit may too often be found in our feelings and language towards our fellow-worshipers and fellow-men. Would you know if this really is so? - just listen to the way in which Churches and Christians often speak of one another. How little of the meekness and gentleness of Jesus is to be seen. It is so little remembered that deep humility must be the keynote of what the servants of Jesus say of themselves or each other. Is there not many a Church or assembly of the saints, many a mission or convention, many a society or committee, even many a mission away in heathendom, where the harmony has been disturbed and the work of God hindered, because men who are counted saints have proved in touchiness and haste and impatience, in self-defense and self-assertion, in sharp judgments and unkind words, that they did not each reckon others better than themselves, and that their holiness has but little in it of the meekness of the saints? In their spiritual history men may have had times of great humbling and brokenness, but what a different thing this is from being clothed with humility, from having an humble spirit, from having that lowliness of mind in which each counts himself the servant of others, and so shows forth the very mind which was also in Jesus Christ.

"Stand by; for I am holier than thou!" What a parody on holiness! Jesus the Holy One is the humble One: the holiest will ever be the humblest. There is none holy but God: we have as much of holiness as we have of God. And according to what we have of God will be our real humility, because humility is nothing but the disappearance of self in the vision that God is all. The holiest will be the humblest. Alas! Though the bare-faced boasting Jew of the days of Isaiah is not often to be found, even our manners have taught us not to speak thus, how often this spirit is still seen, whether in the treatment of fellow-saints or of the children of the world. In the spirit in which opinions are given, and work is undertaken, and faults are exposed, how often, though the clothes be that of the publican, the voice is still that of the Pharisee: "Oh God, I thank Thee that I am not as other men."

And is there, then, such humility to be found, that men shall indeed still count themselves "less than the least of all saints," the servants of all? There is. "Love vaunteth not itself, is not puffed up, seeketh not its own."

Where the spirit of love is shed abroad in the heart, where the divine nature comes to a full birth where Christ the meek and lowly Lamb of God is truly formed within, there is given the power of a perfect love that forgets itself and finds its blessedness in blessing others, in bearing with them and honoring them, however feeble they be. Where this love enters, there God enters. And where God has entered in His power, and reveals Himself as All, there the creature becomes nothing. And where the creature becomes nothing before God; it cannot be anything but humble towards the fellow-creature. The presence of God becomes not a thing of times and seasons, but the covering under which the soul ever dwells, and its deep humiliation before God becomes the holy place of His presence from where all its words and works proceed.

May God teach us that our thoughts and words and feelings concerning our fellow-men are His test of our humility towards Him, and that our humility before Him is the only power that can enable us to be always humble with our fellow-men. Our humility must be the life of Christ, the Lamb of God, within us. Let all teachers of holiness, whether in the pulpit or on the platform, and all seekers after holiness, whether in the closet or the convention, take warning. There is no pride so dangerous, because none so subtle and insidious, as the pride of holiness. It is not that a man ever says, or even thinks, "Stand by; I am holier than thou." No, indeed, the thought would be regarded with abhorrence. But there grows up, all unconsciously, a hidden habit of soul, which feels complacency in its attainments, and cannot help seeing how far it is in advance of others. It can be recognized, not always in any special self-assertion or self-applause, but simply in the absence of that deep self-humiliation which cannot but be the mark of the soul that has seen the glory of God (Job 42: 5, 6; Isa.6: 5). It reveals itself, not only in words or thoughts, but in a tone, a way of speaking of others, in which those who have the gift of spiritual discernment cannot but recognize the power of self. Even the world with its keen eyes notices it, and points to it as a proof that the profession of a heavenly life does not bear any special heavenly fruits. O brethren, beware! Unless we make, with each advance in what we think is holiness, the increase of humility our study, we may find that we have been delighting in beautiful thoughts and feelings, in solemn acts of consecration and faith, while the only sure mark of the presence of God, the disappearance of self, was all the time wanting. Come and let us flee to Jesus, and hide ourselves in Him until we be clothed upon with His humility. That alone is our holiness.

Chapter 8

Humility and Sin

"Sinners, of whom I am chief." 1 Tim.1:15

Humility is often identified with penitence (regret / repentance) and contrition (remorse / sorrow). As a consequence, there appears to be no way of fostering humility but by keeping the soul occupied with its sin. We have learned, I think, that humility is something else and something more. We have seen in the teaching of our Lord Jesus and the Epistles how often the virtue is mentioned without any reference to sin. In the very nature of things, in the whole relation of the creature to the Creator, in the life of Jesus as He lived it and imparts it to us, humility is the very essence of holiness as of blessedness. It is the displacement of self by the enthronement of God. Where God is all, self is nothing.
But though it is this aspect of the truth I have felt it specially needful to press, I need hardly say what new depth and intensity man's sin and God's grace give to the humility of the saints. We have only to look at a man like the Apostle Paul, to see how, through his life as a ransomed and a holy man, the deep consciousness of having been a sinner lives inextinguishably. We all know the passages in which he refers to his life as a persecutor and blasphemer. "I am the least of the apostles, that am not worthy to be called an apostle, because I persecuted the Church of God ...I labored more abundantly than they all; yet not I, but the grace of God which was with me" (I Cor. 15: 9,10). "Unto me, who am less than the least of

all saints, was this grace given, to preach to the heathen" (Eph.3: 8). "I was before a blasphemer, and a persecutor, and injurious; howbeit I obtained mercy, because I did it ignorantly in unbelief ...Christ Jesus came into the world to save sinners, of whom I am chief" (1 Tim.1:13,15). God's grace had saved him; God remembered his sins no more for ever; but never, never could he forget how terribly he had sinned. The more he rejoiced in God's salvation, and the more his experience of God's grace filled him with joy unspeakable, the clearer was his consciousness that he was a saved sinner, and that salvation had no meaning or sweetness except as the sense of his being a sinner made it precious and real to him. Never for a moment could he forget that it was a sinner God had taken up in His arms and crowned with His love.

The texts we have just quoted are often appealed to as Paul's confession of daily sinning. One has only to read them carefully in their context, to see how little this is the case. They have a far deeper meaning, they refer to that which lasts throughout eternity, and which will give its deep undertone of amazement and adoration to the humility with which the ransomed bow before the throne, as those who have been washed from their sins in the blood of the Lamb. Never, never, even in glory, can they be other than ransomed sinners; never for a moment in this life can God's child live in the full light of His love, but as he feels that the sin, out of which he has been saved, is his only right and title to all that grace has promised to do. The humility with which first he came as a sinner, acquires a new meaning when he learns how it becomes him as a creature. And then ever again, the humility, in which he was born as a creature, has its deepest and richest tones of adoration, in the memory of what it is to be a monument of God's wondrous redeeming love.

The true importance of what these expressions of St. Paul teach us comes out all the more strongly when we notice the remarkable fact that, through his whole Christian course, we never find from his pen, even in those epistles in which we have the most intensely personal unbosoming's, anything like confession of sin. Nowhere is there any mention of shortcoming or defect, nowhere any suggestion to his readers that he has failed in duty, or sinned against the law of perfect love. On the contrary, there are passages not a few in which he vindicates himself in language that means nothing, if it does not appeal to a faultless life before God and men.

"Ye are witnesses and God also, how holily, and righteously, and un-blamably we behaved ourselves toward you" (1 Thess.2:10). "Our glorying is this, this testimony of our conscience, that in holiness and sincerity of God we behaved ourselves in the world, and more abundantly to you ward" (2Cor.1:12). This is not an ideal or an aspiration; it is an appeal to what his actual life had been. However we may account for this absence of confession of sin, all will admit that it must point to a life in the power of the Holy Ghost, such as is but seldom realized or expected.

The point which I wish to emphasize is this; that the very fact of the absence of such confession of sinning only gives the more force to the truth that it is not in daily sinning that the secret of the deeper humility will be found, but in the habitual, never for a moment to be forgotten position, which just the more abundant grace will keep more distinctly alive, that our only place, the only place of blessing, our one abiding position before God, must be that of those whose highest joy it is to confess that they are sinners saved by grace. With Paul's deep remembrance of having sinned so terribly in the past, before grace had met him, and the consciousness of being kept from present sinning, there was ever coupled the abiding remembrance of the dark hidden power of sin ever ready to come in, and only kept out by the presence and power of the indwelling Christ. "In me, that is, in my flesh, dwelleth no good thing;" these words of Rom. 7 describe the flesh as it is to the end. The glorious deliverance of Rom.8 "The law of the Spirit of life in Christ Jesus hath now made me free from the law of sin, which once led me captive" is neither the annihilation nor the sanctification of the flesh, but a continuous victory given by the Spirit as He mortifies the deeds of the body.

As health expels disease, and light swallows up darkness, and life conquers death, the indwelling of Christ through the Spirit is the health and light and life of the soul. But with this, the conviction of helplessness and danger ever tempers the faith in the momentary and unbroken action of the Holy Spirit into that chastened sense of dependence which makes the highest faith and joy the handmaids of a humility that only lives by the grace of God. The three passages above quoted all show that it was the wonderful grace bestowed upon Paul, and of which he felt the need every moment, that humbled him so deeply. The grace of God that was with him, and enabled him to labor more abundantly than they all; the grace to preach to the heathen the unsearchable riches of Christ; the grace that was exceeding abundant with faith and love which is in Christ Jesus, it was this grace of which it is the very nature and glory that it is for sinners, that kept the consciousness of his having once sinned, and being liable to sin, so intensely alive. "Where sin abounded, grace did abound more exceedingly."

This reveals how the very essence of grace is to deal with, and take away sin. It is not sin, but God's grace showing a man and ever reminding him what a sinner he was, that, will keep him truly humble. It is not sin, but grace, that will make me indeed know myself a sinner, and make the sinner's place of deepest self-denial the place I never leave.

I fear that there are not a few who, by strong expressions of self-condemnation and self-denunciation, have sought to humble themselves, and have to confess with sorrow that a humble spirit, a "heart of humility," with its accompaniments of kindness and compassion, of meekness and forbearance, is still as far off as ever. Being occupied with self, even amid the deepest self-abhorrence, can never free us from self. It is the revelation of God, not only by the law condemning sin but by His grace delivering us from it that will make us humble. The law may break the heart with fear; it is only grace that works that sweet humility which becomes a joy to the soul as its second nature. It was the revelation of God in His holiness, drawing close to make Himself known in His grace that made Abraham and Jacob, Job and Isaiah, bow so low. It is the soul in which God the Creator, as the All of the creature in its nothingness, God the Redeemer in

His grace, as the All of the sinner in his sinfulness, is waited for and trusted and worshiped, that will find itself so filled with His presence, that there will be no place for self. So alone can the promise be fulfilled: "The haughtiness of man shall be brought low, and the Lord alone be exalted in that day." It is the sinner dwelling in the full light of God's holy, redeeming love, in the experience of that full indwelling of divine love, which comes through Christ and the Holy Spirit, who cannot but be humble. Not to be occupied with thy sin, but to be occupied with God, brings deliverance from self.

Chapter 9

Humility and Faith

"How can ye believe, which receive glory from one another, and the glory that cometh from the only God ye seek not?" John 5: 44

In an address I lately heard, the speaker said that the blessings of the higher Christian life were often like the objects exposed in a shop window, one could see them clearly and yet could not reach them. If told to stretch out his hand and take, a man would answer, I cannot; there is a thick pane of plate-glass between me and them. And even so Christians may see clearly the blessed promises of perfect peace and rest, of overflowing love and joy, of abiding communion and fruitfulness, and yet feel that there was something between hindering the true possession. And what might that be? Nothing but pride. The promises made to faith are so free and sure; the invitations and encouragements so strong; the mighty power of God on which it may count is so near and free, that it can only be something that hinders faith that hinders the blessing being ours. In our text Jesus reveals to us that it is indeed pride that makes faith impossible. "How can ye believe, which receive glory from one another?" As we see how in their very nature pride and faith are irreconcilably at variance, we shall learn that faith and humility are at the root one, and that we never can have more of true faith than we have of true humility; we shall see that we may indeed have strong intellectual conviction and assurance of the truth while pride is kept in the heart, but that it makes the living faith, which has power with God, an impossibility.

We need only think for a moment what faith is. Is it not the confession of nothingness and helplessness, the surrender and the waiting to let God work? Is it not in itself the most humbling thing there can be, the acceptance of our place as dependents, who can claim or get or do nothing but what grace bestows?! Humility is simply the disposition which prepares the soul for living on trust. And every, even the most secret breathing of pride, in self-seeking, self-will, self-confidence, or self-exaltation, is just the strengthening of that self which cannot enter the kingdom, or possess the things of the kingdom, because it refuses to allow God to be what He is and must be there, the All in All.

Faith is the organ or sense for the perception and apprehension of the heavenly world and its blessings. Faith seeks the glory that comes from God, that only comes where God is All. As long as we take glory from one another, as long as ever we seek and love and jealously guard the glory of this life, the honor and reputation that comes from men, we do not seek, and cannot receive the glory that comes from God. Pride renders faith impossible. Salvation comes through a cross and a crucified Christ. Salvation is the fellowship with the crucified Christ in the Spirit of His cross. Salvation is union with and delight and participation in the humility of Jesus. Is it a wonder that our faith is so feeble when pride still reigns so much, and we have hardly learnt even to long or pray for humility as the most needful and blessed part of salvation? Humility and faith are more closely allied in Scripture than many know. See it in the life of Christ. There are two cases in which He spoke of a great faith. Had not the centurion, at whose faith He marveled, saying, "I have not found so great faith, no, not in Israel!" spoken, "I am not worthy that Thou should come under my roof"? And had not the mother to whom He spoke, "O woman, great is thy faith!" accepted the name of dog, and said, "Yea, Lord, yet the dogs eat of the crumbs'? It is the humility that brings a soul to be nothing before

God, that also removes every hindrance to faith, and makes it only fear lest it should dishonor Him by not trusting Him wholly.

Beloved, have we not here the cause of failure in the pursuit of holiness? Is it not this, though we knew it not, that made our consecration and our faith so superficial and so short-lived? We had no idea to what an extent pride and self were still secretly working within us, and how alone God by His incoming and His mighty power could cast them out. We understood not how nothing but the new and divine nature, taking entirely the place of the old self, could make us really humble. We knew not that absolute, unceasing, universal humility must be the root-disposition of every prayer and every approach to God as well as of every dealing with man; and that we might as well attempt to see without eyes, or live without breath, as believe or draw close to God or dwell in His love, without an all-pervading humility and lowliness of heart.

Beloved, have we not been making a mistake in taking so much trouble to believe, while all the time there was the old self in its pride seeking to possess itself of God's blessing and riches? No wonder we could not believe. Let us change our course. Let us seek first of all to humble ourselves under the mighty hand of God: He will exalt us. The cross, and the death, and the grave, into which Jesus humbled Himself, were His path to the

glory of God. And they are our path. Let our one desire and our fervent prayer be, to be humbled with Him and like Him; let us accept gladly whatever can humble us before God or men; this alone is the path to the glory of God.

You perhaps feel inclined to ask a question. I have spoken of some who have blessed experiences, or are the means of bringing blessing to others, and yet are lacking in humility. You ask whether these do not prove that they have true, even strong faith, though they show too clearly that they still seek too much the honor that comes from men. More than one answer can be given. But the principal answer in our present connection is this: They indeed have a measure of faith, in proportion to which, with the special gifts bestowed upon them, is the blessing they bring to others. But in that very blessing the work of their faith is hindered, through the lack of humility. The blessing is often superficial or transitory, just because they are not the nothing that opens the way for God to be all. A deeper humility would without doubt bring a deeper and fuller blessing. The Holy Spirit not only working in them as a Spirit of power, but dwelling in them in the fullness of His grace, and specially that of humility, would through them communicate Himself to these converts for a life of power and holiness and steadfastness, now all too little seen. "How can ye believe, which receive glory from one another?" Beloved! - nothing can cure you of the desire of receiving glory from men, or of the sensitiveness and pain and anger which come when it is not given, but giving yourself to seek only the glory that comes from God. Let the glory of the All-glorious God be everything to you. You will be freed from the glory of men and of self, and be content and glad to be nothing.

Out of this nothingness you will grow strong in faith, giving glory to God, and you will find that the deeper you sink in humility before Him, the nearer He is to fulfill the every desire of your Faith.

Chapter 10

Humility and Death to Self

"He humbled Himself and became obedient unto death." Phil.2: 8.

Humility is the path to death, because in death it gives the highest proof of its perfection. Humility is the blossom of which death to self, is the perfect fruit. Jesus humbled Himself unto death, and opened the path in which we too must walk. As there was no way for Him to prove His surrender to God to the very uttermost, or to give up and rise out of our human nature to the glory of the Father but through death, so with us too.

Humility must lead us to die to self; so we prove how wholly we have given ourselves up to it and to God; so alone we are freed from fallen nature, and find the path that leads to life in God, to that full birth of the new nature, of which humility is the breath and joy.

We have spoken of what Jesus did for His disciples when He communicated His resurrection life to them, when in the descent of the Holy Spirit He, the glorified and enthroned Meekness actually came from heaven Himself to dwell in them. He won the power to do this through death: in its inmost nature the life He imparted was a life out of death, a life that had been surrendered to death, and been won through death. He who came to dwell in them was Himself One who had been dead and now lives for evermore. His life, His person, His presence, bear the marks of death, of being a life begotten out of death. That life in His disciples ever bears the death-marks too; it is only as the Spirit of the death, of the dying One, dwells and works in the soul, that the power of His life can be known. The first and chief of the marks of the dying of the Lord Jesus, of the death-marks that show the true follower of Jesus, is humility. For these two reasons: Only humility leads to perfect death; only death perfects humility. Humility and death are in their very nature one: humility is the bud; in death the fruit is ripened to perfection.

Humility leads to perfect death. Humility means the giving up of self and the taking of the place of perfect nothingness before God. Jesus humbled Himself, and became obedient unto death. In death He gave the highest, the perfect proof of having given up His will to the will of God. In death He gave up His self, with its natural reluctance to drink the cup; He gave up the life He had in union with our human nature; He died to self, and the sin that tempted Him; so, as man, He entered into the perfect life of God. If it had not been for His boundless humility, counting Himself as nothing except as a servant to do and suffer the will of God, He never would have died.

This gives us the answer to the question so often asked, and of which the meaning is so seldom clearly apprehended: How can I die to self? The death to self is not your work, it is God's work. In Christ you are dead to sin. The life there is in you, has gone through the process of death and resurrection; you may be sure you are indeed dead to sin. But the full manifestation of the power of this death in your disposition and conduct depends upon the measure in which the Holy Spirit imparts the power of the death of Christ, and here it is that the teaching is needed: if you would enter into full fellowship with Christ in His death, and know the full deliverance from self, humble yourself. This is your one duty. Place yourself before God in your utter helplessness; consent heartily to the fact of your impotence to slay or make alive yourself; sink down into your own nothingness, in the spirit of meek and patient and trustful surrender to God. Accept every humiliation, look upon every fellow-man who tries or annoy you, as a means of grace to humble you.

Use every opportunity of humbling yourself before your fellow-men as a help to abide humbly before God. God will accept such humbling of yourself as the proof that your whole heart desires it, as the very best prayer for it, as your preparation for His mighty work of grace, when, by the mighty strengthening of His Holy Spirit, He reveals Christ fully in you, so that He, in His form of a servant, is truly formed in you, and dwells in your heart. It is the path of humility which leads to perfect death, the full and perfect experience that we are dead in Christ.

Then follows: Only this death leads to perfect humility. Oh, beware of the mistake so many make, who would eagerly be humble, but are afraid to be too humble. They have so many qualifications and limitations, so many reasoning's and questionings, as to what true humility is to be and to do, that they never unreservedly yield themselves to it. Beware of this. Humble yourself unto the death. It is in the death to self that humility is perfected. Be sure that at the root of all real experience of more grace, of all true advance in consecration, of all actually increasing conformity to the likeness of Jesus, there must be a deadness to self that proves itself to God and men in our dispositions and habits. It is sadly possible to speak of the death-life and the Spirit-walk, while even the tenderest love cannot but see how much there is of self. The death to self has no surer death-mark than a humility which makes itself of no reputation, which empties out itself, and takes the form of a servant. It is possible to speak much and honestly of fellowship with a despised and rejected Jesus, and of bearing His cross, while the meek and lowly, the kind and gentle humility of the Lamb of God is not seen, is scarcely sought. The Lamb of God means two things, meekness and death. Let us seek to receive Him in both forms. In Him they are inseparable: they must be in us too.

What a hopeless task if we had to do the work! Nature never can overcome nature, not even with the help of grace. Self can never cast out self, even in the regenerate man. Praise God, the work has been done, and finished and perfected forever. The death of Jesus, once and forever, is our death to self. And the ascension of Jesus, His entering once and for ever into the Holiest, has given us the Holy Spirit to communicate to us in power, and make our very own, the power of the death-life. As the soul, in the pursuit and practice of humility, follows in the steps of Jesus, its consciousness of the need of something more is awakened, its desire and hope is quickened, its faith is strengthened, and it learns to look up and claim and receive that true fullness of the Spirit of Jesus, which can daily maintain His death to self and sin in its full power, and make humility the all-pervading spirit of our life.(See note at end of this chapter.)

"Are ye ignorant that all we who were baptized into Jesus Christ were baptized into His death? Reckon yourselves to be dead unto sin, but alive unto God in Christ Jesus. Present yourself unto God, as alive from the dead. "The whole self-consciousness of the Christian is to be filled and characterized by the spirit that animated the death of Christ. He has ever to present himself to God as one who has died in Christ, and in

Christ is alive from the dead, bearing about in his body the dying of the Lord Jesus. His life ever bears the two-fold mark: its roots striking in true humility deep into the grave of Jesus, the death to sin and self; its head lifted up in resurrection power to the heaven where Jesus is.

Believer, claim in faith the death and the life of Jesus as thine. Enter in His grave, into the rest from self and its work, into the rest of God. With Christ, who committed His spirit into the Father's hands, humble thyself and descend each day into that perfect, helpless dependence upon God. God will raise thee up and exalt thee. Sink every morning in deep, deep nothingness into the grave of Jesus; every day the life of Jesus will be manifest in thee. Let a willing, loving, restful, happy humility be the mark that thou hast indeed claimed thy birthright; the baptism into the death of Christ. "By one offering He has perfected forever them that are sanctified. "The souls that enter into His humiliation will find in Him the power to see and count self dead, and, as those who have learned and received of Him, to walk with all lowliness and meekness, forbearing one another in love. The death-life is seen in a meekness and lowliness like that of Christ.

Note: "To die to self, or come from under its power, is not, cannot be done, by any active resistance we can make to it by the powers of nature. The one true way of dying to self is the way of patience, meekness, humility, and resignation to God. This is the truth and perfection of dying to self. For if I ask you what the Lamb of God means, must you not tell me that it is and means the perfection of patience, meekness, humility, and resignation to God? Must you not therefore say that a desire and faith in these virtues is an application to Christ, is a giving up yourself to Him and the perfection of faith in Him? And then, because this inclination of your heart to sink down in patience, meekness, humility, and resignation to God, is truly giving up all that you are and all that you have from fallen Adam, it is perfectly leaving all you have to follow Christ; it is your highest act of faith in Him. Christ is nowhere but in these virtues; when they are there, He is in His own kingdom. Let this be the Christ you follow.

"The Spirit of divine love can have no birth in any fallen creature, until it wills and chooses to be dead to all self, in a patient, humble resignation to the power and mercy of God. "I seek for all my salvation through the merits and mediation of the meek, humble, patient, suffering Lamb of God, who alone hath power to bring forth the blessed birth of these heavenly virtues in my soul. There is no possibility of salvation but in and by the birth of the meek, humble, patient, resigned Lamb of God in our souls. When the Lamb of God hath brought forth a real birth of His own meekness, humility, and full resignation to God in our souls, then it is the birthday of the Spirit of love in our souls, which, whenever we attain, will feast our souls with such peace and joy in God as will blot out the remembrance of everything that we called peace or joy before.
"This way to God is infallible. This infallibility is grounded in the twofold character of our Savior: 1. As He is the Lamb of God, a principle of all meekness and humility in the soul; 2. As He is the Light of heaven, and blesses eternal nature, and turns it into a kingdom of heaven. When we are willing to get rest for our souls in meek, humble resignation to God, then it is that He, as the Light

of God and heaven, joyfully breaks in upon us, turns our darkness into light, and begins that kingdom of God and of love within us, which will never have an end." William Law

Chapter 11

Humility and Happiness

"Most gladly therefore will I rather glory in my weaknesses, that the strength of Christ may rest upon me. Wherefore I take pleasure in weakness: for when I am weak then am I strong." 2Cor.12:9,10.

Lest Paul should exalt himself, by reason of the exceeding greatness of the revelations, a thorn in the flesh was sent him to keep him humble. Paul's first desire was to have it removed, and he besought the Lord three times that it might depart. The answer came that the trial was a blessing; that, in the weakness and humiliation it brought, the grace and strength of the Lord could be the better manifested. Paul at once entered upon a new stage in his relation to the trial: instead of simply enduring it, he most gladly gloried in it; instead of asking for deliverance, he took pleasure in it. He had learned that the place of humiliation is the place of blessing, of power, and joy.
Every Christian virtually passes through these two stages in his pursuit of humility. In the first he fears and flees and seeks deliverance from all that can humble him. He has not yet learnt to seek humility at any cost. He has accepted the command to be humble, and seeks to obey it, though only to find how utterly he fails. He prays for humility, at times

very earnestly; but in his secret heart he prays more, if not in word, then in wish, to be kept from the very things that will make him humble. He is not yet so in love with humility as the beauty of the Lamb of God, and the joy of heaven, that he would sell all to procure it. In his pursuit of it, and his prayer for it, there is still somewhat of a sense of burden and of bondage; to humble himself has not yet become the spontaneous expression of a life and a nature that is essentially humble. It has not yet become his joy and only pleasure. He cannot yet say, "Most gladly do I glory in weakness, I take pleasure in whatever humbles me."

But can we hope to reach the stage in which this will be the case? Undoubtedly. And what will it be that brings us there? That which brought Paul there, a new revelation of the Lord Jesus. Nothing but the presence of God can reveal and expel self. A clearer insight was to be given to Paul into the deep truth that the presence of Jesus will banish every desire to seek anything in ourselves, and will make us delight in every humiliation that prepares us for His fuller manifestation. Our humiliations lead us, in the experience of the presence and power of Jesus, to choose humility as our highest blessing. Let us try to learn the lessons the story of Paul teaches us.

We may have advanced believers, eminent teachers, men of heavenly experiences, who have not yet fully learnt the lesson of perfect humility, gladly glorying in weakness. We see this in Paul. The danger of exalting himself was coming very near. He knew not yet perfectly what it was to be nothing; to die, that Christ alone might live in him; to take pleasure in all that brought him low. It appears as if this was the highest lesson that he had to learn, full conformity to his Lord in that self-emptying where he gloried in weakness that God might be all.

The highest lesson a believer has to learn is humility. Oh that every Christian who seek to advance in holiness may remember this well! There may be intense consecration, and fervent zeal and heavenly experience, and yet, if it is not prevented by very special dealings of the Lord, there may be an unconscious self-exaltation with it all. Let us learn the lesson, the highest holiness is the deepest humility; and let us remember that comes not of itself, but only as it is made a matter of special dealing on the part of our faithful Lord and His faithful servant.

Let us look at our lives in the light of this experience, and see whether we gladly glory in weakness, whether we take pleasure, as Paul did, in injuries, in necessities, in distresses. Yes, let us ask whether we have learnt to regard a reproof, just or unjust, a reproach from friend or enemy, an injury, or trouble, or difficulty into which others bring us, as above all an opportunity of proving Jesus is all to us, how our own pleasure or honor are nothing, and how humiliation is in very truth what we take pleasure in. It is indeed blessed, the deep happiness of heaven, to be so free from self that whatever is said of us or done to us is lost and swallowed up, in the thought that Jesus is all.

Let us trust Him who took charge of Paul to take charge of us too. Paul needed special discipline, and with it special instruction, to learn, what was more precious than even the unutterable things he had heard in heaven, what it is to glory in weakness and lowliness. We need it, too, oh so much. He who cared for him will care for us too.

He watches over us with a jealous, loving care, "lest we exalt ourselves". When we are doing so, He seeks to discover to us the evil, and deliver us from it. In trial and weakness and trouble He seeks to bring us low, until we so learn that His grace is all, as to take pleasure in the very thing that brings us and keeps us low. His strength made perfect in our weakness, His presence filling and satisfying our emptiness, becomes the secret of a humility that need never fail. It can, as Paul, in full sight of what God works in us, and through us, ever say, "In nothing was I behind the chiefest apostles, though I am nothing." His humiliations had led him to true humility, with its wonderful gladness and glorying and pleasure in all that humbles.

"Most gladly will I glory in my weaknesses, that the power of Christ may rest upon me; wherefore I take pleasure in weaknesses." The humble man has learnt the secret of abiding gladness. The weaker he feels, the lower he sinks; the greater his humiliations appear, the more the power and the presence of Christ are his portion, until, as he says, "I am nothing," the word of his Lord brings ever deeper joy: "My grace is sufficient for thee." I feel as if I must once again gather up all in the two lessons: the danger of pride is greater and nearer than we think, and the grace for humility too.

The danger of pride is greater and nearer than we think, and that especially at the time of our highest experiences. The preacher of spiritual truth with an admiring congregation hanging on his lips, the gifted speaker on a Holiness platform expounding the secrets of the heavenly life, the Christian giving testimony to a blessed experience, the evangelist moving on as in triumph, and made a blessing to rejoicing multitudes – no man knows the hidden, the unconscious danger to which these are exposed. Paul was in danger without knowing it; what Jesus did for him is written for our admonition, that we may know our danger and know our only safety. If ever it has been said of a teacher or professor of holiness, he is so full of self; or, he does not practice what he preaches; or, his blessing has not made him humbler or gentler, let it be said no more.

Jesus, in whom we trust, can make us humble. Yes, the grace for humility is greater and nearer, too, than we think. The humility of Jesus is our salvation: Jesus Himself is our humility. Our humility is His care and His work. His grace is sufficient for us, to meet the temptation of pride too. His strength will be perfected in our weakness. Let us choose to be weak, to be low, to be nothing. Let humility be to us joy and gladness. Let us gladly glory and take pleasure in weakness, in all that can humble us and keep us low. The power of Christ will rest upon us. Christ humbled Himself, therefore God exalted Him. Christ will humble us, and keep us humble; let us heartily consent, let us trustfully and joyfully accept all that humbles; the power of Christ will rest upon us. We shall find that the deepest humility is the secret of the truest happiness, of a joy that nothing can destroy.

Chapter 12

Humility and Exaltation

"He that humbleth himself shall be exalted." Luke 14:11, and 18:14. "God giveth grace to the humble. Humble yourself in the sight of the Lord, and He shall exalt you." Jas. 4:10. "Humble yourselves therefore under the mighty hand of God, that He may exalt you in due time." 1 Peter 5:6.

Just yesterday I was asked the question, how am I to conquer this pride? The answer; was simple. Two things are needed. Do what God says is your work: humble yourself. Trust Him to do what He says is His work: He will exalt you. The command is clear: humble yourself. That does not mean that it is your work to conquer and cast out the pride of your nature, and to form within yourself the lowliness of the holy Jesus. No, this is God's work; the very essence of that exaltation, wherein He lifts you up into the real likeness of the beloved Son. What the command does mean is this: take every opportunity of humbling yourself before God and man. In the faith of the grace that is already working in you; in the assurance of the more grace for victory that is coming; up to the light that conscience each time flashes upon the pride of the heart and its workings; notwithstanding all there may be of failure and falling, stand persistently as under the unchanging command: humble yourself. Accept with gratitude everything that God allows from within or without, from friend or enemy, in nature or in grace, to remind you of your need of humbling, and to help you to it.

Reckon humility to be indeed the mother-virtue, your very first duty before God, the one perpetual safeguard of the soul, and set your heart upon it as the source of all blessing. The promise is divine and sure: He that humbleth himself shall be exalted. See that you do the one thing God asks: humble yourself. God will see that He does the one thing He has promised. He will give more grace; He will exalt you in due time.

All God's dealings with man are characterized by two stages. 1) There is the time of preparation, when command and promise, with the mingled experience of effort and impotence, of failure and partial success, with the holy expectancy of something better which these waken, train and discipline men for a higher stage. 2) Then comes the time of fulfillment, when faith inherits the promise, and enjoys what it had so often struggled for in vain. This law holds good in every part of the Christian life, and in the pursuit of every separate virtue, and that because it is grounded in the very nature of things. In all that concerns our redemption, God needs to take the initiative. When that has been done, man's turn comes. In the effort after obedience and attainment, he must learn to know his impotence. In self-despair he must die to himself, and so be fitted voluntarily and intelligently to receive from God the promise, the completion of that which he had accepted in the beginning in ignorance. So, God who had been the Beginning, before man rightly knew Him, or fully understood what His purpose was, is longed for and welcomed as the End, as the All in All.

It is even thus, too, in the pursuit of humility. To every Christian the command comes from the throne of God Himself: humble yourself. The

earnest attempt to listen and obey will be rewarded, yes, rewarded with the painful discovery of two things. The one, what depth of pride, that is of unwillingness to count oneself and to be counted nothing, to submit absolutely to God, there was, that one never knew. The other, what utter
impotence there is in all our efforts, and in all our prayers too for God's help, to destroy the hideous monster.
Blessed is the man who now learns to put his hope in God, and to persevere, notwithstanding all the power of pride within him, in acts of humiliation before God and men. We know the law of human nature: acts produce habits, habits breed dispositions, dispositions form the will, and the rightly-formed will is character. It is not otherwise in the work of grace. As acts, persistently repeated, beget habits and dispositions, and these strengthened the will, He who works both to will and to do, comes with His mighty power and Spirit; and the humbling of the proud heart with which the repentant saint cast himself so often before God, is rewarded with the "more grace" of the humble heart, in which the Spirit of Jesus has conquered, and brought the new nature to its maturity, and He the meek and lowly One now dwells forever.
Humble yourselves in the sight of the Lord, and He will exalt you. And wherein does the exaltation rest? The highest glory of the creature is in being only a vessel, to receive and enjoy and show forth the glory of God. It can do this only as it is willing to be nothing in itself, that God may be all. Water always fills first the lowest places. The lower, the emptier a man lies before God, the speedier and the fuller will be the inflow of the divine glory. The

exaltation God promises is not, cannot be, any external thing apart from Himself; all that He has to give or can give is only more of Himself, Himself to take more complete possession. The exaltation is not, like an earthly prize, something arbitrary, in no necessary connection with the conduct to be rewarded.

No, but it is in its very nature the effect and result of the humbling of ourselves. It is nothing but the gift of such a divine indwelling humility, such conformity to and possession of the humility of the Lamb of God, as fits us for receiving fully the indwelling of God. He that humbleth himself shall be exalted. Of the truth of these words Jesus Himself is the proof; of the certainty of their fulfillment to us He is the pledge. Let us take His yoke upon us and learn of Him, for He is meek and lowly of heart. If we are but willing to stoop to Him, as He has stooped to us, He will yet stoop to each one of us again, and we shall find ourselves not unequally yoked with Him. As we enter deeper into the fellowship of His humiliation, and either humble ourselves or bear the humbling of men, we can count upon it that the Spirit of His exaltation, "the Spirit of God and of glory," will rest upon us. The presence and the power of the glorified Christ will come to them that are of a humble spirit. When God can again have His rightful place in us, He will lift us up. Make His glory your care in humbling yourself; He will make your glory His care in perfecting your humility, and breathing into you, as your abiding life, the very Spirit of His Son. As the all-pervading life of God possesses you, there will be nothing so natural, and nothing so sweet, as to be nothing, with not a thought or wish for self, because all is occupied with Him who filleth all.

"Most gladly will I glory in my weakness, that the strength of Christ may rest upon me. "Beloved, have we not here the reason that our consecration and our faith have availed so little in the pursuit of holiness? It was by self and its strength that the work was done under the name of faith; it was for self and its happiness that God was called in; it was, unconsciously, but still truly, in self and its holiness that the soul rejoiced. We never knew that humility, absolute, abiding, Christ-like humility and self-denial, pervading and marking our whole life with God and man, was the most essential element of the life of the holiness we sought for. It is only in the possession of God that I lose myself. As it is in the height and breadth and glory of the sunshine that the littleness of the mote playing in its beams is seen, even so humility is taking our place in God's presence as nothing but a mote dwelling in the sunlight of His love.

"How great is God! How small am I! Lost, swallowed up in Love's immensity! God only there, not I." May God teach us to believe that to be humble, to be nothing in His presence, is the highest attainment, and the fullest blessing of the Christian life. He speaks to us: "I dwell in the high and holy place, and with him that is of a contrite and humble spirit." Be this our portion! "Oh, to be emptier, lowlier, unnoticed, and unknown, And to God a vessel holier, Filled with Christ, and Christ alone!"

A Secret of Secrets: Humility, the Soul of True Prayer. Till the spirit of the heart be renewed, till it is emptied of all earthly desires, and stands in an habitual hunger and thirst after God, which is the true spirit of prayer; till then, all our prayer will be, more or less, but too much like lessons given to scholars; and we shall mostly say them, only because we dare not neglect them.

But be not discouraged; take the following advice, and then you may go to church without any danger of mere lip-service or hypocrisy, although there should be a hymn or a prayer, whose language is higher than that of your heart. Do this: go to the church as the publican went to the temple; stand inwardly in the spirit of your mind in that form which he outwardly expressed, when he cast down his eyes, and could only say, "God be merciful to me, a sinner." Stand unchangeably, at least in your desire, in this form or state of heart; it will sanctify every petition that comes out of your mouth; and when anything is read or sung or prayed, that is more exalted than your heart is, if you make this an occasion of further sinking down in the spirit of the publican, you will then be helped, and highly blessed, by those prayers and praises which seem only to belong to a heart better than yours.

This, my friend, is a secret of secrets; it will help you to reap where you have not sown, and be a continual source of grace in your soul; for everything that inwardly stirs in you, or outwardly happens to you, becomes a real good to you, if it finds or excites in you this humble state of mind. For nothing is in vain, or without profit to the humble soul; it stands always in a state of divine growth; everything that falls upon it is like a dew of heaven to it. Shut up yourself, therefore, in this form of Humility; all good is enclosed in it; it is a water of heaven, that turns the fire of the fallen soul into the meekness of the divine life, and creates that oil, out of which the love to God and man gets its flame. Be enclosed, therefore, always in it; let it be as a garment wherewith you are always covered, and a girdle with which you are girt; breathe nothing but in and from its spirit; see nothing but with its eyes; hear nothing but with its ears. And then, whether you are in the church or out of the church, hearing the praises of God or receiving wrongs from men and the world, all will be edification, and everything will help forward your growth in the life of God - a Prayer for Humility. I will here give you an infallible touchstone that will try all to the truth. It is this: retire from the world and all conversation, only for one month; neither write, nor read, nor debate anything with yourself; stop all the former workings of your heart and mind: and, with all the strength of your heart, stand all this month, as continually as you can, in the following form of prayer to God. Offer it frequently on your knees; but whether sitting, walking, or standing, be always inwardly longing, and earnestly praying this one prayer to God: "That of His great goodness He would make known to you, and take from your heart, every kind and form and degree of Pride, whether it be from evil spirits, or your own corrupt nature; and that He would awaken in you the deepest depth and truth of that Humility, which can make you capable of His light and Holy Spirit." Reject every thought, but that of waiting and praying in this matter from the bottom of your heart, with such truth and earnestness, as people in torment wish to pray and be delivered from it ... If you can and will give yourself up in truth and sincerity to this spirit of prayer, I will venture to affirm that, if you had twice as many evil spirits in you as Mary Magdalene had, they will all be cast out of you, and you will be forced with her to weep tears of love at the feet of the holy Jesus.

Notes
* "All this is to make it known the region of eternity that pride can degrade the highest angels into devils, and humility raise fallen flesh and blood to the thrones of angels. Thus, this is the great end of God raising a new creation out of a fallen kingdom of angels: for this end it stands in its state of war between the fire and pride of fallen angels, and the humility of the Lamb of God, that the last trumpet may sound the great truth through the depths of eternity, that evil can have no beginning but from pride, and no end but from humility. The truth is this: Pride may die in you, or nothing of heaven can live in you. Under the banner of the truth, give yourself up to the meek and humble spirit of the holy Jesus. Humility must sow seed, or there can be no reaping in Heaven. Look not at pride only as an unbecoming temper, nor at humility only as a decent virtue: for the one is death, and the other is life; the one is all hell, the other is all heaven. So much as you have of pride within you, you have of the fallen angels alive in you; so much as you have of true humility, so much you have of the Lamb of God within you. Could you see what every stirring of pride does to your soul, you would beg of everything you meet to tear the viper from you, though with the loss of a hand or an eye. Could you see what a sweet, divine, transforming power there is in humility, how it expels the poison of your nature, and makes room for the Spirit of God to live in you, you would rather wish to be the footstool of all the world than

want the smallest degree of it." Spirit of Prayer, Pt.II, p.73, Edition of Moreton, Canterbury, 1893.

* "We need to know two things: 1) That our salvation consists wholly in being saved from ourselves, or that which we are by nature; 2) That in the whole nature of things, nothing could be this salvation or savior to us, but such a humility of God as is beyond all expression. Hence the first unalterable term of the Savior to fallen man: Except a man denies himself, he cannot be My disciple. Self is the whole evil of fallen nature; self-denial is our capacity of being saved; humility is our savior ... Self is the root, the branches, the tree, of all the evil of our fallen state. All the evils of fallen angels and men have their birth in the pride of self. On the other hand, all the virtues of the heavenly life are the virtues of humility. It is humility alone that makes the unpassable gulf between heaven and hell. What is then, or in what lies, the great struggle for eternal life? It all lies in the strife between pride and humility: pride and humility are the two master powers, the two kingdoms in strife for the eternal possession of man. There never was, nor ever will be, but one humility, and that is the one humility of Christ. Pride and self have the all of man, till man has his all from Christ. He therefore only fights the good fight whose strife is that the self-idolatrous nature which he hath from Adam may be brought to death by the supernatural humility of Christ brought to life in him." W. Law, Address to the Clergy, p. 52. [I hope that this book of Law on the Holy Spirit may be issued by my publisher in the course of the year.]

A free e-book from http://manybooks.net/. This is the website where you can download Andrew Murray's book about Humility.

Epilogue

After completing this book, I became aware of even more pride in myself. It is as if a magnifying glass runs up and down me. Beloved, let us not be discouraged. The only time one can fix something is when you become aware that it is broken. Support, pray, encourage each other and walk the path of faith. God Himself will be our comforter. Earnestly pray for the gift of the discerning of spirits 1Co 12:10.

www.ingramcontent.com/pod-product-compliance
Lightning Source LLC
Chambersburg PA
CBHW061324040426
42444CB00011B/2759